Ready for Anything

*Supporting New Teachers
for Success*

Ready for Anything

Supporting New Teachers for Success

Lynn F. Howard

A L P
Advanced
Learning
Press

A L P
Advanced
Learning
Press

Advanced Learning Press

317 Inverness Way South, Suite 150
Englewood, CO 80112
Phone (800) 844-6599 or (303) 504-9312 ■ Fax (303) 504-9417
www.AdvancedLearningPress.com

Library of Congress Cataloging-in-Publication Data

Howard, Lynn F., 1954–
    Ready for anything : supporting new teachers for success / Lynn F. Howard
      p. cm.
  Includes bibliographical references.
   ISBN-13: 978-0-9747343-8-5
   ISBN-10: 0-9747343-8-1
   1. First year teachers—In-service training—United States. 2. Teacher
effectiveness—United States. I. Title.
LB2844.1.N4H69 2006
371.1—dc22   2005057208

Printed in the United States of America

10 09 08 07 06   01 02 03 04 05 06 07 08 09

Dedication

Most of us have had a special teacher who made a difference in our lives. Mr. Tucker was a wonderful high school teacher, and I became a science educator because of him. There was something magical about Mr. Tucker that none of us quite understood, but we were always anxious to get to his classes. I met Mr. Tucker when I entered the ninth grade, and I ended up taking every biology, oceanography, and science course he taught. With colored chalk in hand and thousands of pages of notes, we learned everything there was to know about cells, invertebrates, and creepy-crawlies. Mr. Tucker taught us far more than science content: he instilled in us a love of learning and the passion to always believe in ourselves and our aspirations. Mr. Tucker touched the lives of thousands of children, and I hope that every child will be inspired by such an educator. As teachers, whether veteran or rookie, it is our job to make it happen for our students: today, tomorrow, and forever.

Contents

Preface

I HAVE THE DUBIOUS HONOR OF (probably)
holding a world record—one that most likely will never make
it into the *Guinness Book of World Records*. I was in Seattle in
late October of 1995 for a board meeting with a professional
organization. We had visited Mount St. Helens in 1985, five years
after the initial eruption, and I wanted to take photographs of the
environmental changes to share with my earth science classes.
I collected my backpack and camera and started up the road to
Mount St. Helens in my rental car. It began to rain, the tempera-
ture dropped into the thirties, and the fog became so thick that
I couldn't see the hood of the car. While driving the 21 miles to
the summit view, I did not see any living thing, nor did I see any
other cars—not even road kill!

I realized that the rapidly deteriorating weather would make it
impossible for me to take the photos I had wanted. I parked
the car next to a sign that welcomed me to Mount St. Helens, took
that one picture, and decided to return to Seattle. It was dark
and sleeting when I pulled into a turnout that offered a series of
portable toilets that were being winterized for the season. I took
my car key (but not the backpack), entered one of these modern
outhouses, and closed the door. That was when I heard a quiet but
terrifying noise, as the latch on the outside clicked down. I was
locked in with no hope of rescue, no materials or utensils (except
the car key), and no technology!

Although the experience of being locked in an outhouse is rare (most of us never have this particular opportunity), prior experience and expertise give each of us the ability to solve problems and react positively. Not having acquired the necessary skills and expertise puts one at a tremendous disadvantage, as I discovered while locked in that outhouse 21 miles from civilization. I'm not likely to forget the feeling of despair and disaster that came over me then.

I use this experience as an analogy for new teachers, relating the fear, loneliness, and sense of total helplessness to being in a classroom on the first day of school. This book is about the survival of a beginning teacher and how schools can provide ongoing support and help to create qualified educators. I have a passion for new teachers; you may never meet anyone who is more dedicated and committed to the success of each one. To that end, I spent hours talking to educators and researching to find out what teacher induction practices were effective, yet user-friendly for the new educator. I found that to really help retain new educators, individual schools, rather than districts, should take responsibility for supporting and building competent and qualified teachers.

I did, and I made a difference!

P.S.: For the rest of the story, see the "Final Thoughts" section at the end of this book!

Acknowledgments

A Special Thank-You

My husband quit a wonderful job after we had been married for three years, and announced that he wanted to be a teacher. I laughed and asked just what he thought he might teach. He decided that he might want to coach, but it didn't really matter to him, so I invited him to visit my junior high science classes. He stayed seven minutes and decided that he would be better suited to elementary school students. After teaching first and second grades, he found his love in kindergarten, where he has taught over 20 years. Through more than 30 years of marriage, I acknowledge his dedication and commitment to following his dream. Teachers have a calling to this profession, and I truly believe that passion and the love of children are the only reasons to go into education. My husband has been my reality check, always reminding me that if it doesn't work in kindergarten, it just won't work.

Thank you, Wallace!

Other Acknowledgments

This book is about new teachers and the conversations that I have had with them, their principals, their colleagues, and their students. Part of the purpose of this book is to recognize the numerous hours that we spent crying and celebrating, yelling and thinking, and finding solutions to every problem that confronts a first-year teacher. It is impossible to name everyone, but a special smile goes to John, McKinley, Jarma, and every new teacher I had the opportunity to meet and talk with around the country. You helped me realize that our responsibility is to make each and every one of you successful.

Thanks go especially to Catherine, for without her desire and passion to become a teacher, none of this would have been possible. It was through her continued quest for teaching excellence that *Ready for Anything* evolved. I know that if every new teacher had the commitment and dedication to students that Catherine constantly demonstrates, the future of education would be positive and hopeful.

Calvin, I am forever grateful for the opportunity to work with you. You allowed me to go beyond the job description and out on my own to follow my dream and passion for struggling teachers. It was your philosophy that allowed me to do what I do best. You hired well, trusted me, and let me make mistakes and grow. It was the best five years of my professional career. When I grow up, I want to be just like you.

Special appreciation goes to all my colleagues at home and around the country. You allowed me into your districts and schools to work with you and understood that my only role was one of support, respect for your endeavors, and a never-ending pursuit of something better for students. You respected and trusted me and gave me the opportunity to learn from you and work together to build great learning communities. We truly made the difference in the lives of children.

Thanks also to Anne, who made this possible. You saw my passion for new teachers and convinced others that this was the right path to take with publishing. I am eternally grateful for the day we met, your relentless pursuit of this project, and your confidence in the book and in me.

Lastly, I would be remiss if I didn't say how much I appreciate my family and their undying support over the years. I was a lucky child to know that my dreams and inspirations were always encouraged and never questioned. My parents remain my biggest cheerleaders.

About the Author

LYNN HOWARD HAS BEEN IN EDUCATION for more than 30 years, with the Charlotte-Mecklenburg School System and as a consultant for numerous school districts around the country. She taught junior high and middle school science for 18 years, coordinated a middle-school gifted child program, and acted as assistant and instructional specialist to regional superintendents. Lynn has given extensive professional development presentations around the country, bringing a wealth of experience to schools and districts on subjects that include improving planning and teaming, leadership and relationship building, and systematic school reform strategies. Her passion is teacher support. One of her middle school principals said, "Lynn is always welcome at my school because she brings a realistic and teacher-friendly approach to professional development. My teachers know they will take something away that works and can be used the next day in the classroom."

Lynn has presented at national conferences, including ASCD, National Science Teachers, Staff Development for Educators, and the International Reading Association, and has done presentations for many other state and regional organizations.

Lynn holds a bachelor's degree in biology and a master's degree in earth science and education from the University of North Carolina at Charlotte. She has also earned Academy Certification from the National Staff Development Council, and national certification in Gifted and Talented. She presently works with the

Center for Performance Assessment as a professional development associate.

Lynn lives with her husband, who teaches kindergarten, and two cats in Huntersville, North Carolina. Both Lynn and her husband enjoy gardening and traveling, and have only one more state to visit to complete their tour of all 50. As befits someone who survived being locked in an outhouse, Lynn brings an adventurous approach to real-life strategies for teaching and learning.

Introduction

Contents

ARE YOU STRUGGLING WITH TEACHER RETENTION? I assume that if you are reading this book, you perceive a need to improve teacher retention in your district or school.

Ready for Anything: Supporting New Teachers for Success provides a process for teacher retention that has been successful in both schools with high turnover rates and schools with few new teachers. There are numerous formal teacher induction programs across the country, and every district has some type of process or program that is designed to transform a novice, inexperienced person into a competent, qualified educator. Many of these programs are outstanding, providing a balance of support and mentoring for a successful start to an education career. However, none of these programs provides a step-by-step process designed to meet the needs of individual schools and personnel. Too often, new educators are invited into a large assembly hall and welcomed to the wonderful world of teaching, alerted to the district dos and don'ts, and told how happy each of them will be when they meet their students for the first time. Unfortunately, new teachers don't really understand the first-day-of-school "pep talk" until they experience a react-now situation personally. The speech heard before school begins is soon forgotten after the first day with the students, when the reality of the new job begins to sink in and uncertainty becomes the order of the day.

SOME OF US HAVE STOOD AT THE RIM of the Grand Canyon and marveled at the chasm's vastness and beauty. Some of us venture to walk a few steps along the trail and thrill at the rock layers representing billions of years of earth history. A few even travel the trail by four-legged beast. Only those of us who have lost our minds, however, ever walk to the bottom and back out in July. A trip to the bottom of the Grand Canyon is a journey of wonderment and breathtaking sights. For those who survive the trip, the adventure is a test of skill and endurance that leaves images forever embedded in the mind. The canyon trail goes downward for miles, narrowing and becoming treacherous as it overlooks steep dropoffs and cliffs. The toll on the body is tremendous, as heat and dehydration become more intense during the descent. The philosophy of *I've heard about it but haven't done it* applies to a trek into the Grand Canyon. We had read about the canyon, watched videos, listened to ranger talks, and heard stories from those who had ventured into its depths. We stood at the edge of the canyon, looking in with excitement and wonder, full of energy and power. As our journey downward began, we were caught up in the thrill of the moment and ready to see what was at the next turn. Walking down was relatively quick, and rest stops along the way provided some shade as we drank much-needed water. The six-mile trek downward was full of conversation and photo moments.

After hours of walking, we made it to the bottom, celebrating our accomplishment with an apple and some crackers. We turned around to see how far we had come and the reality of what we had done hit hard. What came down had to go back up. The bottom of the canyon represents only a turning point in the journey. We reflected on why we did this and what we needed to walk our way out. No words were said as we struggled back up the same six miles through intense heat, pressure changes, and little water.

A NEW TEACHER STANDS AT THE EDGE of the classroom looking in with excitement and wonder, full of ideas, hopes, and questions. New teachers read about the classroom, watch videos, listen to experts, and talk to veterans, but nothing truly prepares them for the reality of the first year. As the start of the year approaches, it is easy to be caught up in the thrill of being a teacher of children. However, disillusionment and struggle begin as the journey continues; not far into the year, timelines, mandates, and lack of knowledge fill the space where enthusiasm once thrived. No matter how much someone tells you about classroom management, organization, and relationships, it is not enough until you have the actual experience of doing it the first time. How are you helping your new teachers survive the canyon?

This Is Not Just Another Book on Teacher Retention

Have you talked to a new teacher on the day before school starts? Have you talked to a new teacher in December? Is there a difference? What happens from day one to the middle of the year? New teachers come to school excited, wanting to save the world. Do you remember your first day of teaching? There was nothing you couldn't do and no child you couldn't teach. Given all this, why is there such quick disillusionment with the teaching profession? First-year teachers are pressed into the service of the day-to-day duties and responsibilities assigned by the building administrators and district mandates. They are more likely than not to be assigned to low-performing students, required to "float" through classrooms, and given extra duties. In addition, they often come into the profession with no formal training, from an outside business or profession.

I remember my first day of teaching. College and student teaching had prepared me, I thought, and I was really excited, energetic, and eager to share my love of science with my students. By the time that first day had come and gone, I had survived with no books, no desks, 8 periods, and 182 students. It was a wonderful feeling. I hadn't hurt anyone, yelled at anyone, or done anything that would be perceived as bad, and I was coming back tomorrow.

Do you remember your first day of teaching? There was nothing you couldn't do and no child you couldn't teach. Given all this, why is there such quick disillusionment with the teaching profession?

Mr. Brawley, who taught next door, had been cordially introduced. At the end of the day, he threw open my door, inquired how my day had been, and said, "You have only 5,999 days until you can retire." I sat down and cried.

It is to Mr. Brawley that I say thanks: for reminding me that for a new teacher, it is the day-to-day, and more likely hour-to-hour, survival that builds the skills and knowledge needed for success. I will never forget our 15 years together, and although I did not appreciate Mr. Brawley at that first moment, I have treasured and respected his friendship and support over the past 30 years.

Why Did You Go into Education?

If you reflect back, the reason you went into education was probably that you wanted to make a difference with children. Maybe you dreamed of being a teacher, and even played "teacher" as a child in anticipation of having your own classroom full of eager students. I remember the day I told my mother, who taught English, that I would never, ever, no-way-in-a-million-years, teach school. I wanted to go to medical school and become a pathologist.

That was my dream, but it never happened. I think my mother knew that it wouldn't work, even though I had spent my entire life playing scientist. During my college years, I had the opportunity to work in a juvenile delinquency center in Atlanta. For some strange reason, I felt a kinship with the 18 young men there, aged 13 to 17, all of whom had had numerous altercations with the law. I spent a lot of time with Billy, who was in the center for derailing a train. He taught me to play pool and showed me that to win, you must have a strategic plan, skill, and knowledge to get all the balls to go where you want them to go. I learned how to talk "street" and discovered that the gut level of survival is the only thing that makes a life-and-death difference. I really liked Billy and know that my time with him provided insights into reality that I would never have gotten in another job. I reflect back on this and believe that the premise of *Ready for Anything: Supporting New Teachers for Success* came from Billy's lessons in life.

If you reflect back, the reason you went into education was probably that you wanted to make a difference with children. Maybe you dreamed of being a teacher . . . of having your own classroom full of eager students.

After marrying and moving to North Carolina, I decided that I needed a job, so I finished a degree in secondary science education. The summer after graduation, I was offered a job by the principal of the local junior high school. I thought it would be simple: How hard could it be to teach eighth-graders?

Would You Want to Be a New Teacher Today?

Veteran educators give mixed answers to the question: Would you want to be a new teacher today? With the endless barrage of countless challenges that children bring to the classroom, many teachers have to pause to reflect before answering this question. When a group of experienced teachers was asked to brainstorm all the roles, responsibilities, and "things" that a new teacher has to learn, they generated a list of more than 100 items. Take a minute to think about selected tasks and decide what you could do well on your very first day.

lesson design	lack of time	exceptional children
language barriers	health issues	funding
INTASC Standards	strategies	support
retention	collaboration	turnover
stress	flexibility	organization
IEPs	testing	licensure
procedures	PTSA	grades
planning	mentors	reflections
attendance	climate	lunch duty
homework	schedule	paycheck
assessments	AV equipment	standards
report cards	parents	paperwork
monitoring	ill students	data analysis

When a group of experienced teachers was asked to brainstorm all the roles, responsibilities, and "things" that a new teacher has to learn, they generated a list of more than 100 items.

What Is *Ready for Anything: Supporting New Teachers for Success?*

Ready for Anything: Supporting New Teachers for Success is a year-long, site-based process that provides skills and strategies to build the confidence and experience necessary for new teachers to grow professionally at the beginning of this new career. The program focuses on one guiding question: *Are you having the same problems?*

This ongoing, professional development support program gives new teachers an opportunity to explore methods and activities that answer their questions and meet their needs. It was created through years of personal experience, talk with struggling new staff and experienced educators, and advice from former students. These strategies may be perceived by veterans as too easy, but a new teacher needs a step-by-step guide to survival, not a one-shot meeting in August about benefits and retirement. The framework of the *Ready for Anything* program is a series of seminars (usually held monthly) that are based on best practices and supply easy-to-implement activities that new teachers can use in their classrooms right away.

The Rationale

It is far better to retain a savable teacher than to train new ones year after year! The challenge for schools is to implement and sustain a year-long, intensive support program that: (1) supports the vision and mission of the school district and the school, (2) focuses on and implements best instructional practices, and (3) places a value on professional development. "Teacher expertise is the most important factor in determining student achievement. The most effective and efficient way to increase the number of competent teachers is through high-quality, comprehensive professional development" (Darling-Hammond & Bell, 1997).

The No Child Left Behind Act of 2002 (NCLB) requires that every class be taught by a "highly qualified teacher"; it also requires academic achievement by every student in every school. If we recognize that teacher quality is the greatest predictor of student success, we see that the need to develop and implement a well-designed support program could not be more critical. Despite the challenges that come with teaching, most new educators are given little professional support or ongoing guidance. At a time when educational quality tops the public's list of concerns, classrooms across the United States continue to suffer serious teacher shortages.

The shortage is exacerbated by the fact that new teachers are at high risk of leaving, even though it typically takes three to six years to develop a competent teacher. New teachers usually find that they are unprepared for the reality of the classroom. According to national exit surveys, teachers typically express "disillusionment with the job," along with numerous other reasons why teachers leave the profession:

- Lack of support from administrators
- Not feeling valued
- Too much paperwork and not enough time
- Inadequate salary and benefits
- Relocation and family commitment

The result is that new teachers leave the field at an alarming rate. In fact, 14 percent leave by the end of their first year, 33 percent leave within 3 years, and 50 percent leave within 5 years (Ingersoll, 2003).

Recognizing and understanding these identified barriers, and addressing each of them, should be the integral focus of a strong retention program. Analyzing and implementing an action plan is an obligation and an opportunity for a school to significantly improve teacher retention.

Two components make *Ready for Anything: Supporting New Teachers for Success* different from traditional teacher retention models:

1. **The process design is totally site-based.** It is developed and implemented according to the needs and composition of the current teaching staff. Conversations regarding the program are held prior to implementation so that there is a schoolwide commitment to the process and its philosophy. The integrity, culture, and dignity of the school and district are never compromised. Facilitation and implementation are owned by the stakeholders at the school level.

Ready for Anything: Supporting New Teachers for Success is a year-long, site-based process that provides skills and strategies to build the confidence and experience necessary for new teachers to grow professionally at the beginning of this new career.

2. **Implementation of the model is ongoing.** Lateral-entry camps, mentors, weekend workshops, and after-school sessions do not provide the continuous support and contact that new teachers have told us make the difference. Monthly seminars and weekly support from the administrative team, facilitators, mentors, and support personnel form the backbone, and are critical for the success, of the program. The strategies and activities are modeled through research-based effective teaching and professional development standards.

The Goal

Ready for Anything: Supporting New Teachers for Success has only one goal: to have a teacher want to return to the same school next year. The ownership of teacher retention should be site-based and provide a continuous, seamless flow of professional development targeted at skill and knowledge development for new teachers. New teachers must have close access to support from the school administration and a nonevaluative facilitator to improve their instructional expertise in curriculum skills, management, and classroom presentation. *Ready for Anything: Supporting New Teachers for Success* is designed to:

- Provide new teachers with sustained professional development that is relevant, standards-based, and job-embedded.
- Supply new teachers with instructional strategies, including management, instruction, and assessment.
- Give administrators a collaborative support model for new teachers.
- Improve the level of teacher satisfaction regarding instruction, management, working conditions, and school climate.
- Raise student achievement through teacher capacity building.
- Build capacity through a site-based program that will sustain itself.

Adult Learners

One of the major benefits of *Ready for Anything: Supporting New Teachers for Success* is that the process is site-based, developed to meet individual school needs, and managed by a facilitator who is in the school building. Part of the development process for this program involved understanding how adults learn, and always

Ready for Anything: Supporting New Teachers for Success has only one goal: to have a teacher want to return to the same school next year.

remembering that each individual learns differently and with his or her own style. Several specific characteristics of adult learners were considered during development of *Ready for Anything: Supporting New Teachers for Success:*

1. **All adults have prior knowledge related to education.** These experiences are excellent points of reference as new teachers develop new skills and knowledge. The advantage is that adults can share previous experiences about teaching and learning, which can be used as discussion points in each seminar.

2. **Adults have a purpose for learning new information.** In the case of the new teacher, this information, along with the new skills and strategies, provides the framework for success in the classroom. Adult learners need to know the why and the how before they are willing to take a chance on a new strategy or activity.

3. **Adults want to be respected and appreciated for who they are and what they bring to the group.** Opportunities for celebrating success, in a professional manner, will build positive relationships and foster the development of trust and confidence as new teachers grow and learn.

4. **Adult learners want to know the expectations and the requirements.** New teachers both desire and are committed to do their best, and they set high goals as long as there is a reason for learning something new. The work must be applicable to their individual situations, so it falls to the instructor to demonstrate and prove the relevance of seminar classroom assignments.

5. **Adult learners want to be social.** All new teachers want to make new friends, understand that they are not alone, and watch how others deal with similar situations. They need to process information by talking to and sharing ideas with others. The seminars should provide opportunities for new staff to learn collaboratively and become resources for each other.

6. **Adult learners need an appropriate level of difficulty in tasks and assignments.** There should be some challenge, but not at a level that creates unnecessary stress or frustration. Each seminar should have intense modeling and explanations so that the tasks are clearly understood and readily undertaken.

7. **Adult learners want feedback from peers and supervisors.** They want the opportunity to observe others, return to their own classrooms and practice, and receive advice from someone

All new teachers want to make new friends, understand that they are not alone, and watch how others deal with similar situations. They need to process information by talking to and sharing ideas with others. The seminars should provide opportunities for new staff to learn collaboratively and become resources for each other.

they view as an expert in the field. A simple note of thanks and a word of encouragement are powerful motivators to new teachers. The ultimate achievement is to gain personal advancement—in this case, returning to the school next year with stronger skills and knowledge and a commitment to professional development and student achievement.

Who Benefits?

The ultimate stakeholder in a teacher retention program is the student, who gets better teachers and hence better achievement opportunities. The program builds teaching capacity through teachers' active participation in the seminars. *Ready for Anything: Supporting New Teachers for Success* targets new staff, but the principal has the flexibility to offer the program to other staff members as well, based on their performance needs. Veteran teachers can stop by to get a new instructional strategy or network with other teachers.

The Content

Ready for Anything: Supporting New Teachers for Success is about what new teachers need to manage a classroom from day one until the end of the school year. As we interviewed new teachers about their concerns and issues, a long list of barriers to success emerged. An analysis of the list targets specific logistics, skills, and knowledge areas that are not acquired through experience or educational preparation courses. The seminars were developed based on these topics:

- An understanding of the new process of opening school
- The difficulty of organizing time and work
- Inadequate preparation in instructional strategies
- Large class sizes
- Lack of materials and resources (including classrooms)
- Paperwork
- Lack of respect or recognition
- Lack of time to plan and work collaboratively
- Extracurricular duties

The ultimate stakeholder in a teacher retention program is the student, who gets better teachers and hence better achievement opportunities.

Ready for Anything: Supporting New Teachers for Success is about what new teachers need to manage a classroom from day one until the end of the school year.

Are You Having the Same Problem?

A single question is the premise of *Ready for Anything: Supporting New Teachers for Success:* "Are you having the same problem?" The benefit of these periodic seminars is that new staff members learn that they are not alone; they find that they are experiencing the same issues and concerns as others. Over and over, we heard that this was the most valuable component of the seminars; because of this, many of the new staff made it through the year understanding that they were not failures or isolated cases. In addition, teachers acquired skills in small steps, and had time to practice and master the strategies before formal observations and evaluations were done. Conference time with the facilitator, either individually or in small groups, reconfirmed the facts that all the teachers were going through a learning process and that it takes time to develop a teaching style and effective performance.

The INTASC Standards

Ready for Anything: Supporting New Teachers for Success was developed around what effective teachers should know and be able to do. The program is founded on the implementation of strategies and activities that are both performance-based and in line with the National Board approach to standards development. In creating the *Ready for Anything: Supporting New Teachers for Success* model, we discovered that it was important to find a common core of teaching skills and knowledge that could be correlated with student success and achievement.

The Interstate New Teacher Assessment and Support Consortium (INTASC) provided a framework for the skills and knowledge base that all new teachers should have. The INTASC Standards (*figure A*) are embedded in the *Ready for Anything: Supporting New Teachers for Success* seminars. Seminar 1 gives an overview of the 10 standards, and Seminar 6 gives a more detailed explanation of each. In addition, *figures 6.4* through *6.8* set out checklists of "Evidence of Effective Teaching" regarding management of time, behavior, instruction, monitoring and feedback, and non-instructional duties; these worksheets supplement the INTASC Standards as teachers prepare for observations and evaluations.

The following 10 standards reflect what novice teachers should know and be able to do in the following areas:

1. Content Pedagogy
2. Student Development
3. Diverse Learners
4. Multiple Instructional Strategies
5. Motivation and Management
6. Communication and Technology
7. Planning
8. Assessment
9. Reflective Practice: Professional Development
10. School and Community Involvement

(Permission for inclusion granted by the Council of Chief State School Officers (1992).)

In creating the *Ready for Anything: Supporting New Teachers for Success* model, we discovered that it was important to find a common core of teaching skills and knowledge that could be correlated with student success and achievement.

How to Use This Book

Contents

What Will You Find in This Book?

This book is simple to use. Seminars 1 through 11 present the logistical and content information for 11 facilitated seminars, with prepared materials and strategies that can either be used as is or changed and revised as needed for each individual school setting. Strategies and activities incorporate the best instructional practices and the most relevant information to date. Personal stories related to each topic are included to reinforce the reality of the new educator's career; facilitators should feel free to include their own experiences and expertise for each topic. Following the seminars, a separate section, addressed to the school principal, provides strategies and ideas for extending the *Ready for Anything: Supporting New Teachers for Success* program at the principal's site. Additional resources are listed at the end of the book.

This book provides tried-and-true, teacher-tested tips, ideas, and strategies to help you with the first year. It supplies a wealth of practical, easy-to-implement strategies and activities for managing and organizing time, developing good relationships, and creating effective lessons.

What Will You *Not* Find in This Book?

The book presents a format for creating a site-based teacher support program. It does not contain every possible strategy, idea, method, or suggestion for new teacher success; rather, it sets out a systematic process that is designed to be used and expanded. It does not guarantee 100 percent teacher retention, but it does provide a plan for improving the chances of retention at your school. Multiple activities, both for the facilitator and for the classroom teacher, are the framework of the process. The *Ready for Anything: Supporting New Teachers for Success* program is not an all-inclusive list of skills and knowledge that new teachers need, but it targets and collects the crucial proficiencies that all new teachers need to be successful.

How to Begin

If you are the *superintendent of the district,* ask yourself: "How can I improve teacher retention in my district?" You understand the need for a teacher retention program in your schools, and you are responsible for leading your principals in an effective implementation program. Take the time to analyze the current teacher retention numbers, and commit to implementing an effective program that can be differentiated and revised based on individual school and staff needs. Your year-long administrative planning calendar should contain time for principals to meet and discuss the fundamentals of the program and decide what specific, site-based resources and materials are required.

If you are the *principal of a school,* ask yourself: "Do I retain teachers, or do I have to recruit each year?" All educators and administrators understand that some people simply were not created to be teachers; these individuals should select another career. The principal must decide if an individual is worth the fairly substantial investment of time and resources needed to yield a competent and qualified educator. Remember, though, that *you* are the number-one reason that new teachers say they leave a school. Every new educator wants to see and have access to the boss; new teachers also want to know that they are becoming integral components of the school community.

If you are the *facilitator*, ask yourself: "How well do I remember my first year, and what can I do to make a difference with new teachers?" You have the most important job of all. You will run the *Ready for Anything* program by obtaining the materials, conducting the seminars, providing feedback through nonevaluative observations, and being the primary contact for new staff members. Your role is to give nonthreatening, 100 percent support and guidance.

If you are the *new teacher*, ask yourself: "Am I having the same problems as other new teachers?" You will find the answer to be an unequivocal *yes.* This book provides tried-and-true, teacher-tested tips, ideas, and strategies to help you with the first year. It supplies a wealth of practical, easy-to-implement strategies and activities for managing and organizing time, developing good relationships, and creating effective lessons. All are based on research and best instructional models. Use the reproducibles from these seminars to build your instructional portfolio, and next year, you will find that you are more prepared, more confident, and more ready to deal with the second year.

What Really Matters?

All the new teachers I have met over the years have said that two things would have made the difference in their decision to leave. The first is visibility of the principal at the school site. The second is being able to talk to other new teachers. The question, "Are you having the same problem?," is the underlying theme of the *Ready for Anything* seminars. You have to have the skills and knowledge *before* you need them. New staff who go through this program adopt an "Everything Is a First" philosophy, while realizing that the things that happen are not unique to them alone. For example, I got a call late one night from one of my new teachers, who was excited that she had survived a "first" that day: a fourth-grader's projectile vomiting in the classroom. The teacher was thrilled that she had known the custodian's name and properly handled the occurrence. Such incidents constitute the gut-level things that we so seldom think about sharing with others. We celebrated this success at the next seminar and the teacher received the "Everything Is a First" award for the month.

WHETHER A SCHOOL HAS ONE or many new teachers, the ongoing, site-based support and guidance that the school provides for its new staff are the most critical factor in teacher retention. Your answers to the following guiding questions will indicate your need for this program:

- Who are the new teachers at my school, and how am I responsible for their success and retention?
- Who is going to provide year-long, school-based support for the new staff?
- How and when will this be accomplished?
- What outcomes will be achieved through implementation?

Before beginning a new teacher program or process, take a few minutes to analyze the existing program at your school site. Be reflective and honest and decide if you need to focus on new teacher support, and at what level (see the following chart).

	Low Level	Average Level	High Level
School-based new-teacher support program			
Classroom visits by principal			
Periodic (usually monthly) seminars on relevant topics, providing useful strategies			
Continuous conversations about classroom management			
Modeling and implementation of instructional lesson design			
Strategic planning with standards and objectives			
Stress management program			
Information about testing			
Professional development on school/classroom climate and building relationships			
Plans for celebrations and success			

ARE THERE AREAS THAT COULD DO with just minor improvements? Are there areas of need where you have not yet reached the implementation stage? If the answer in every area is at the high level of implementation, use the materials in this book to supplement and enhance your present program. If you find that your responses reveal low levels of implementation, take the book, copy the reproducibles, set up the program, and get started.

Across the country, schools have multiple induction and mentoring programs, each with a variety of descriptions and characteristics. *Induction programs* are the activities and strategies used to grow a novice teacher into the status of proficient educator. Effective and successful induction programs include orientation, inservices and workshops, professional development planning, mentoring, instructional observations, and peer support groups. A *mentor* is an individual designated to provide support and ongoing collaboration as the new teacher develops the skills and knowledge needed for success. Although *Ready for Anything: Supporting New Teachers for Success* does not formally address the mentoring component of an induction program, it is highly advisable to include mentoring in the overall professional development plan for new staff.

Every district refers to new, beginning, lateral, inexperienced, and rookie teachers with different terms. This book uses many of these terms interchangeably, though the term *new* has multiple meanings. For purposes of this book, a *new teacher* or a *beginning teacher* is one:

- with no prior background or experience.
- with certification and college coursework, but just hired.
- with experience, but just hired by a different district or school system.

You should make an individual determination as to which teachers would benefit most from the program at your school.

Each seminar is based on the skills and knowledge needed to develop qualified teachers. Countless conversations with new staff, veterans, and students provided the content topics for each seminar.

Whether a school has one or many new teachers, the ongoing, site-based support and guidance that the school provides for its new staff are the most critical factor in teacher retention.

Frequently Asked Questions

The following section answers some common questions, and makes suggestions for implementing *Ready for Anything: Supporting New Teachers for Success*. Although the list is not all-inclusive, it covers the essentials for getting started and answers the logistical questions about the program.

Welcome to the Seminars

What are the seminars?

The seminars, which are best held monthly, provide the support and resources needed to improve the skills and knowledge of first-year teachers. More importantly, they are times for new staff to network and share success and frustration stories with other educators who have the same concerns and are experiencing the same problems. Each seminar is an opportunity for the facilitator to share interaction strategies and provide specific methods for immediate use in the classroom. Although each seminar has a specific topic, the school-based team should be flexible in making modifications and changes as needed for a particular school or topic. The *Ready for Anything* seminars are designed to be complete in themselves; they do not require additional time or paperwork from new teachers.

How were the seminars developed?

Each seminar is based on the skills and knowledge needed to develop qualified teachers. Countless conversations with new staff, veterans, and students provided the content topics for each seminar. The INTASC Standards (*figure A*) integrated into the seminars formed the framework for what effective teachers should know and be able to do.

What specific terms are used in this book?

After Three survey—Participant survey related to the implementation and logistics of the *Ready for Anything* program; given after every third seminar. Information should be used by the new-teacher executive committee for program review and revisions.

agenda—Gives the topics for discussion at each seminar.

facilitator strategies—Interactive strategies used by the facilitator to reinforce a topic; methods designed to promote networking and interaction among the new teachers. These strategies are introduced and led by the facilitator or a team of teachers. Each is focused on specific skills and knowledge acquisition related to new-teacher professional growth. Many of the strategies require additional materials (handouts, manipulative supplies, etc.), which are listed in the "Materials" checklist in each seminar.

"I'm Ready for Anything" Self-Assessment—Questions related to the seminar strategies and activities; individual teachers analyze and discuss these items with the facilitator.

INTASC—Interstate New Teacher Assessment Support Consortium.

invitation—Gives the time, date, location, and topic of the seminar.

lesson plan notebook—Three-ring binder/notebook given to each participant at the first seminar; contains lesson plans for the entire year.

new-teacher binder—Three-ring binder/notebook with tabs for each seminar, given to each participant at the first seminar; contains all the materials and resources provided with *Ready for Anything: Supporting New Teachers for Success*.

new-teacher executive committee—A designated group of individuals, including the principal and the facilitator, that meets to discuss the progress of the *Ready for Anything* program, make adjustments based on seminar evaluations, and determine next steps or revisions.

participant—A person who attends the seminars.

reflection—Interactive thinking/reflection activity that supplements the topic and content of each seminar.

reproducibles—Master pages that can be photocopied, reprinted, made into transparencies, or otherwise reproduced for use in facilitator strategies and teacher-directed student activities.

seminar overview—Participant handout, identified by seminar number and title, that outlines the seminar agenda, topics, focus, and INTASC Standard.

Special Request form—Template for a teacher's request for a classroom observation time or needed supplies or assistance.

teacher—Scholar, instructor, student advocate, professional, leader, learner, collaborator, educator.

teacher-directed student activities—Activities (and accompanying reproducibles) provided and modeled during a seminar; intended for immediate use in the classroom with students.

Each seminar is an opportunity for the facilitator to share interaction strategies and provide specific methods for immediate use in the classroom. Although each seminar has a specific topic, the school-based team should be flexible in making modifications and changes as needed for a particular school or topic.

Throughout the book, *Ready for Anything: Supporting New Teachers for Success* includes numerous checklists and essential questions related to the components of effective schools. Each should be used as a starting point—not a replacement—for discussions of standards and accountability, as new teachers gain the skills and knowledge needed to become great educators.

What are the norms for the seminars?

Each seminar should be professional and productive. Establish a set of norms in the beginning so that the time spent is used to a maximum advantage. Suggested norms include the following:

1. Start and end on time and follow the agenda.
2. Attend all meetings.
3. Make decisions through consensus.
4. Withhold judgment.
5. Don't interrupt others.
6. Ask for help and offer help, as needed.
7. Notice and celebrate what has been done well.
8. Let everyone have a chance to speak.

What about district, state, and local accountability standards?

School districts around the country have established standards and objectives for student achievement and learning, evaluation of instructional leaders and teachers, and school improvement planning. Throughout the book, *Ready for Anything: Supporting New Teachers for Success* includes numerous checklists and essential questions related to the components of effective schools. Each should be used as a starting point—not a replacement—for discussions of standards and accountability, as new teachers gain the skills and knowledge needed to become great educators.

Do we still need our mentoring program?

That decision is best left to your district's discretion. If you have both the *Ready for Anything: Supporting New Teachers for Success* program and mentors, spend time with the new-teacher executive committee planning collaboration between the two. You can never give too much help to new teachers, but the messages and information from all programs should be aligned and consistent.

Setting Up the Seminars

The Logistics

What do we need for each seminar?

Each seminar uses the same format, to ensure consistency in planning and implementation. Use the seminar planning checklist (*figure C*) to plan with and to make sure that materials are ready for each participant prior to the scheduled meeting. Before each seminar, read ahead and review the materials needed for the facilitator strategies and teacher-directed student activities so that you have everything ready and know that supplies are easily accessible.

What kind of seminar planner/calendar should we develop?

A planning calendar of seminars and topics (*figure B*) targets identified new-teacher professional development areas. Each month a new topic is introduced, along with discussion of the corresponding INTASC Standard. New teachers need numerous skills and knowledge areas to become master educators, and trying to find the perfect organization of the topics is difficult. In the *Ready for Anything* program, after the first seminar, the school-based team has the flexibility to alter the arrangement of any seminar based on the needs and characteristics of the school. Strategies from the "Principals' Corner" section should also be included in the planning calendar, so that new teachers are alerted to and prepared to attend special events held by the new-teacher executive committee.

What is the time frame for each seminar?

The first seminar should be a full day. This allows time to share, collect materials, model strategies, and reflect. Based on your schedule, add breaks, snack time, and stretch moments. The other monthly seminars should run about two hours each. Use the first 10 to 15 minutes for socializing and networking among the new teachers.

Where are the seminars held?

The seminars should be held in a comfortable area of the school away from the classrooms. If you combine several schools for a workshop, rotate the location among those schools. You must

New teachers need numerous skills and knowledge areas to become master educators, and trying to find the perfect organization of the topics is difficult. In the *Ready for Anything* program, after the first seminar, the school-based team has the flexibility to alter the arrangement of any seminar based on the needs and characteristics of the school.

decide on the time for the seminars; facilitators often choose a common planning time or a time after school hours. Consider the district and schoolwide planning calendar when selecting a day of the week on which to conduct the meetings. It is important that participants have the year-long calendar at the first seminar so that they can plan, organize their time, and integrate their personal lives with school requirements.

What are the seminar reproducibles?

Each seminar has the same format and design. All include an invitation, seminar overview, strategy page(s), reflections, and an "I'm Ready for Anything" Self-Assessment. Examples and reproducibles of each of these are provided for each seminar. Reproducibles for use with facilitator strategies are marked with a compass icon; those for use in teacher-directed student activities bear a pencil icon.

How should the invitation and seminar overview page look?

One of my new teachers collected all the seminar invitations, notes, cartoons, and articles and created a "Wall of Hope" in the back corner behind his desk. It was colorful and bright and constantly reminded him that he really could be a teacher. Use as much color and decorative paper as possible when providing copies of reproducibles for the new-teacher binder.

How early should the invitation and seminar overview page be delivered?

The invitation and seminar overview page for each seminar should be delivered to the new teacher at least one week before the meeting date. At the first seminar, give new teachers the year-long calendar of dates, times, and locations so that they can make plans and schedules in advance.

How should each seminar begin?

The first 10 to 15 minutes of each seminar should be a time for refreshments and socializing among the new teachers. Take a few minutes to ask for questions, concerns, and discussion. Be careful not to allow the opening minutes to develop into a gripe session; rather, channel personal issues through use of the Special Request form.

The Materials

What kind of budget will we need?

As you plan *Ready for Anything: Supporting New Teachers for Success*, consider the cost of producing the program at your site. Although there is no limit to the amount that you could spend for the program, the following components *must* be provided to ensure an effective implementation process:

- General seminar materials
- New-teacher binder with seminar tabs
- Lesson plan notebook for first session
- Plain copy paper
- Decorative paper for invitations
- Copier-quality reproducibles (best kept in sheet protectors)
- General supplies: markers, chart paper, cardstock, tape, and so on
- Printing or photocopying capabilities
- Invitation
- Seminar overview
- Facilitator strategies with accompanying reproducibles
- Teacher-directed student activities with accompanying reproducibles
- Seminar reflections
- Seminar "I'm Ready for Anything" Self-Assessment
- Special Request form (*figure D*)
- Strategy materials (determined by the individual seminar strategy)
- Make-and-take seminar materials (determined by the individual seminar)
- Refreshments (food, paper products, drinks)
- Door prizes

What kind of refreshments should be provided?

Food is the number-one necessity at *all* seminars. The types of refreshments may depend on your budget. The first seminar should be food-plentiful, with breakfast, lunch, and snacks during the day. Seminar 5 and the last seminar should be festive—a time to celebrate with food and fun. For most seminars, it is appropriate to provide light snacks with a mixture of high-calorie and low-fat,

Each seminar has the same format and design. All include an invitation, seminar overview, strategy page(s), reflections, and an "I'm Ready for Anything" Self-Assessment. Examples and reproducibles of each of these are provided for each seminar.

sweet and salty items, soda and fruit juices, and a variety of packaged foods. Community grocery stores are often willing to donate or reduce the cost of refreshments if they know that the items are being used in a school activity. Remember to have paper products and utensils available, provide ice, and make arrangements to dispose of leftover food.

What handouts are required for each participant?

Before the seminar, each participant gets a seminar invitation and seminar overview page. At the seminar itself, they receive:

- Teacher-directed student activities pages with reproducibles
- Reflections
- Seminar "I'm Ready for Anything" Self-Assessment
- *After Three* survey forms (only after Seminars 3, 6, and 9)

Are door prizes necessary for each seminar?

Yes! New teachers enter the profession with few supplies or materials. Door prizes are fun and should be awarded by randomly calling individual names. The number of door prizes you can give out depends on your budget and the availability of suitable items.

What kinds of door prizes are suggested?

Practically any small item that a teacher could use, especially if it can be used in the classroom, is a potential door prize. Suggested items include: small tool kits, free oil changes, plants, hole punches, lotion, hand sanitizers, overhead marker pens, sewing kits, snacks, free class coverage coupons, tissues, flashlights, conference registrations, substitute days while the teacher is doing observations, timers, pencils, dessert coupons, educational membership subscriptions, and bulletin board materials. Use your imagination and experience and develop your own repertoire of prize items.

Where do we get door prizes?

Be creative: ask, beg, and don't take no for an answer. Community partnerships can often provide funds or materials if you explain what you need, what the materials are for, and why you want help. Supermarkets, discount stores, local food vendors, and teacher catalogs offer an endless supply of things needed by new teachers.

Door prizes are fun and should be awarded by randomly calling individual names. The number of door prizes you can give out depends on your budget and the availability of suitable items.

New teachers appreciate even the smallest tokens of generosity; nothing you give will be wasted!

Why do we need a new-teacher binder?

New teachers struggle with organization and management of time, classroom facilities, and student behavior. The new-teacher binder provides a place for all seminar and resource materials collected throughout the year.

Before the first seminar, purchase a large three-ring binder, with seminar tabs, for each new teacher. Print an attractive label with the teacher's name, school, and the date for the front cover. Make sure that teachers bring their binders to every seminar so that they can quickly insert the materials under the appropriate tab. You will find that teachers won't use their binders much the first year—but they will return the following year with a portfolio of ready-to-implement strategies and activities in their lesson plans!

Why do we need a lesson plan binder?

Lesson plans, especially when mandated by the district or school, are always a struggle for new teachers. The lesson plan binder is an organizational tool for compiling a year's worth of information; it makes material easily accessible for use in class or for checking during classroom observations. Several schools that adopted this idea had all teachers use the same color lesson plan binder. Additional tabs may be included for discipline logs, parent contacts, grade sheets, and grade-level planning meeting minutes.

What is the Special Request form?

The Special Request form (*figure D*) is for use by teachers who want additional support or materials. It designates a specific time for the facilitator to visit a class or provide needed supplies. Some new teachers are not comfortable with verbally sharing concerns; this form allows confidentiality while allowing a new teacher to get the help he or she needs.

New teachers struggle with organization and management of time, classroom facilities, and student behavior. The new-teacher binder provides a place for all seminar and resource materials collected throughout the year.

We strongly suggest that a new-teacher executive committee be established to provide integrity, fidelity, and accountability to the *Ready for Anything* process. The principal should lead the group; the committee should include the *Ready for Anything* facilitator, several staff members (including a new teacher), and possibly a community representative.

The People

What is a new-teacher executive committee?

We strongly suggest that a new-teacher executive committee be established to provide integrity, fidelity, and accountability to the *Ready for Anything* process. The principal should lead the group; the committee should include the *Ready for Anything* facilitator, several staff members (including a new teacher), and possibly a community representative.

How often does the new-teacher executive committee meet?

The committee should hold a planning session before implementation of the *Ready for Anything* program and the first seminar. A monthly meeting with the executive committee and the facilitator provides the opportunity to review and revise the program as needed. During this meeting, problems and success stories should be shared with the committee and any concerns addressed.

Why is the facilitator so important?

The facilitator is the person selected to oversee implementation of the *Ready for Anything: Supporting New Teachers for Success* program. The facilitator manages the logistics of the program, including printing and collecting all materials, providing refreshments, conducting classroom observations, and holding individual conferences with each new staff member. This person is also responsible for modeling the strategies and activities so that teachers can effectively implement them in their classrooms. All this requires time, energy, and a strong commitment to the success of new teachers.

The competency and personal skills of the facilitator should create and reinforce a trusting, nonjudgmental relationship with new staff members. It is suggested that time be allocated in the facilitator's regular duty schedule so that he or she can effectively implement the program. The bottom line is that the choice of facilitator makes or breaks the program.

The following delineates the multiple tasks of the facilitator:

- Expertise task (delivers information about the seminar content)
- Planning task (designs the learning environment)

- Instructional task (presents the information, telling participants how and what to do, while modeling the strategy and activity)
- Facilitation task (responds to individual needs and provides support)
- Materials task (provides resources for the seminars and to individual teachers)

What types of strategies and activities form the basis of the seminars?

Facilitator strategies are interactive strategies used by the school-based facilitator to reinforce a topic, promote networking and interaction, and focus on specific skills and knowledge needed by the new teacher. These strategies are introduced and used at the beginning of each seminar. Reproducibles for use with facilitator strategies are marked with a compass icon

Teacher-directed student activities are engagement strategies (with accompanying reproducibles) that classroom teachers can use immediately with their students. The activities are content-generic, require little preparation time, and are appropriate for all grade levels. These activities are modeled by the facilitator during the seminar so that the participants fully understand how to implement the activity. Reproducibles for use in teacher-directed student activities bear a pencil icon.

Who should attend the seminars and when?

Always invite everybody, every time you hold a seminar. Ask the superintendent to drop by for the first session and always keep the central office aware of your calendar. The *Ready for Anything: Supporting New Teachers for Success* program expects the principal to attend each monthly seminar. Remember, new teachers want visibility and support from the top administrator. All your new teachers should be invited to attend the seminars (again, usually held monthly). The executive team should decide if the program is mandatory or voluntary, what exceptions will be made in the case of an absence, and what make-up should be required.

Can other teachers attend the seminars?

Absolutely! I like to post the monthly seminar agenda for the other staff members to see, and have an open-seminar policy if others want to attend to garner new ideas and strategies.

The *Ready for Anything: Supporting New Teachers for Success* program expects the principal to attend each monthly seminar. Remember, new teachers want visibility and support from the top administrator.

Should every participant talk at each seminar?

This depends on the number of participants you have for each seminar. Ideally, you would create an opportunity for everyone to contribute to each of the discussions, but time constraints can be a problem. With a large group, use numerous cooperative learning and networking strategies to allow collaboration and mutual conversations among teachers. It is imperative that you establish an nonthreatening atmosphere in which relationships of trust can flourish.

What if people don't attend?

Your new-teacher executive committee should develop a plan for dealing with new teachers who do not attend the seminars. Make sure that you have a sign-in sheet for each seminar so that you know who attended and can provide the missed materials to each person. Ultimately, the principal makes the final decision on what course of action to take regarding individual participant absences.

How can veteran teachers and students be involved during the year?

An additional panel discussion with veteran teachers and/or students may be incorporated into one of the seminars. Specify a topic and develop related questions around areas such as classroom management, communication, or instructional strategies. Invite selected panel members to join you during the seminar. Always thank these members for their participation.

What do I do with a "problem" new teacher?

The facilitator is the first line of support and guidance for new teachers. Occasionally, though, concerns arise that go beyond the level of the facilitator: these should go directly to the principal. Problems with management, organization, and relationships can be addressed through the administration, leaving the facilitator on at least neutral terms with the staff and keeping the non-evaluative relationships intact. Concerns related to attendance at seminars should be discussed with the new-teacher executive committee.

Seminar Flexibility

How about guest speakers?

Guest speakers are wonderful additions to the seminars. Invite them during the year as determined by availability and seminar content. One of my favorite seminar bonuses was having a former student of mine, who was a deputy sheriff, talk about safety and security before and after school hours. He brought practical knowledge to the meeting and was able to personally relate to each of the participants. Another guest provided foot massage machines for the stress management seminar. Be creative and search out guest visitors to share their stories and expertise with the group.

How are photographs best used?

Photographs are excellent teaching tools. Ideas for classroom arrangements, bulletin boards, and room decor can be shared through pictures of exemplary classrooms. In addition, teachers may use a camera to take pictures of exemplary student behavior to share with the class. Basic procedures, such as walking in a line, being prepared for class, getting attention, and working in a group, can be illustrated through photos. Photos can be made into transparencies or placed on bulletin boards for class viewing.

How is music incorporated into the seminars?

Music is an integral component of the seminars. During refreshment time, music can produce a calming, relaxing effect—especially good at the end of a stressful day! Several of the strategies require the use of music for the beginning or end of an activity, or during a transition between activities. Choose an appropriate type of music and always check with the executive committee before using music in the classroom.

What kind of humor is appropriate?

Cartoons, quotes, stories, and video clips are excellent tools for illustrating a concept or topic, but inoffensiveness, appropriateness, and political correctness are priorities. I suggest that you ask the new-teacher executive committee to review the materials prior to the seminar and offer feedback as to their appropriateness and suitability for your audience. Be aware of cultural norms and the use of material that could be perceived as personally sensitive.

Guest speakers are wonderful additions to the seminars. Invite them during the year as determined by availability and seminar content.

Each seminar covers a specific topic and provides strategies and activities for immediate implementation in the classroom.

How can we unwind and de-stress before each seminar?

Have a basket full of small toys available during the first 10 to 15 minutes of each seminar; socializing and playing help participants unwind and relax after a stressful day. Consider stocking your toy basket with items such as koosh balls, bubbles, tops, balloons, juggling scarves, and noisemakers. Be creative and design your own set of manipulatives.

Can we take new teachers on field trips?

Yes! Get out there to see the communities around the school. One of the best new-teacher field trips is a school-bus ride through the neighborhoods where the students live. Arrange a time to visit feeder schools and exemplary classrooms where teaching is student centered and adult driven.

What type of follow-up should be provided between seminars?

Each seminar covers a specific topic and provides strategies and activities for immediate implementation in the classroom. The facilitator should have a consistent plan to visit every new teacher's classroom once or twice between seminars and give feedback on how the teacher is doing with the new material. At the scheduled conferencing/self-assessment meetings, review areas of growth and areas that need improvement. Notes and comments are always welcome after an observer leaves the room; these provide immediate feedback on what the new teacher is doing with students.

Can the facilitator do anything between the monthly seminars?

Yes! Place a note, poem, article, cartoon, or quote in each teacher's box sometime between seminars. You want each of them to know that someone cares at times other than the monthly seminars. As time permits, design and personalize motivational cards, bookmarks, calendars, and other items with educational sayings and ideas.

Should the participants or facilitator ever leave a comment after a classroom visit?

Yes! A note with a positive comment left on the desk is a wonderful morale booster. If you use a classroom checklist, place it on the desk to be discussed at the self-evaluation conferencing time.

What additional topics might be included?

The seminars are designed to stand alone, with materials, strategies, and activities all included. However, each school and district is unique, and you should take advantage of opportunities to present additional topics as needed. Suggested additions include:

abuse

abusive language

accepting gifts

Adequate Yearly Progress (AYP)

cultural norms

dealing with mentors

diversity

English as a Second Language (ESL)

exceptional children

field trips

food from home

forms

gangs

health/environmental hazards

homework

hostile administrators

Internet usage

No Child Left Behind (NCLB) provisions and requirements

parent conferences

personal safety

phone conversations

policies and procedures

professional organizations

religious holidays

sexual harassment

student pranks

transporting students

understanding the paycheck

unions

weapons

One of the best new-teacher field trips is a school-bus ride through the neighborhoods where the students live. Arrange a time to visit feeder schools and exemplary classrooms where teaching is student centered and adult driven.

Reflecting and Celebrating

Why is the "Reflections" activity important?

The "Reflections" activity at the end of each seminar allows the participant time to process the information learned and think about accomplishments and needs. It is an opportunity to share thoughts and feelings and focus on the overarching question: "Am I having the same problems?"

Each seminar has a different "Reflections" section that correlates to the seminar topic and facilitator strategies. Too often, we require teachers to write pages and pages in journals, to be turned in to a mentor who may or may not read them soon enough to give a timely response. The "Reflections" section serves the same valuable purpose as reviewed journaling, but alleviates paperwork burdens and reduces stress on new teachers while offering time for reflection and thought.

What is the "I'm Ready for Anything" Self-Assessment?

Each seminar contains an "I'm Ready for Anything" Self-Assessment with focused questions related to the specific seminar topic. These questions stimulate thought, reflection, and professional growth as each is addressed with the facilitator during a scheduled individual conference. At this conference, the facilitator and new teacher discuss strengths and areas for improvement and implement a plan to review and guide the teacher's ongoing development.

How do we set up a conferencing schedule?

At the end of each seminar, the facilitator should have each new teacher sign up for a conference time. Have available a calendar with open dates and times that are convenient to both individuals' schedules. Place a reminder in the teacher's box before the conference meeting, reminding him or her of the location and time.

What are the **After Three** *surveys?*

Continuous evaluation and assessment should be integral components of the *Ready for Anything* process. The *After Three* surveys are given to participants at the end of Seminars 3, 6, and 9, with feedback going to the new-teacher executive committee as action items for improvement and possible revision of the program.

Why should we celebrate success?

Because it is the right thing to do. We get caught up in the daily mandates and requirements of the district and school and do not take time just to say thanks for a job well done. *Ready for Anything: Supporting New Teachers for Success* is about the small, incremental steps that build the skills and knowledge needed to make successful teachers. We must recognize the little things that happen every day that make school a good place to be.

How do we measure success?

Success of the program is measured through an analysis of retention data over time, including the percent of teachers who finish the year and return the next year. Anecdotal information is also collected in the form of seminar evaluations, teacher performance observations, and student achievement.

New Teachers, 0–2 Years	% Finishing the Year	% Returning Next Year	% School Turnover	% District Turnover	% State Turnover
Current year					
1 year prior					
2 years prior					

By implementing *Ready for Anything: Supporting New Teachers for Success* at your school site, you are committing to helping and providing a service that builds capacity in new teachers. The process is simple and cost-effective, and the maintenance and implementation are entirely site-based.

Complements to the Seminars

What other resources and educational texts relate to teacher retention?

There is no shortage of good books, models, and texts on teacher induction and retention programs. The materials in the resource list at the end of this book supplement the *Ready for Anything: Supporting New Teachers for Success* program and provide additional strategies and ideas for monthly seminars.

Is this really doable in my school?

Absolutely yes! Every new teacher deserves support and guidance from a program that builds skills and knowledge and provides teachers an opportunity to grow professionally. By implementing *Ready for Anything: Supporting New Teachers for Success* at your school site, you are committing to helping and providing a service that builds capacity in new teachers. The process is simple and cost-effective, and the maintenance and implementation are entirely site-based.

You must make the decision either to recruit or to retain. Start small with the program, and revise it as needed and appropriate for your situation.

INTASC Standards

The Interstate New Teacher Assessment and Support Consortium (INTASC) is a consortium of state educational agencies and national educational organizations dedicated to the reform of the preparation, licensing, and ongoing professional development of teachers. Created in 1987, INTASC's primary constituency is state education agencies responsible for the licensing, program approval, and professional development. Its work is guided by one basic premise: An effective teacher must be able to integrate content knowledge with the specific strengths and needs of students to assure that all students learn and perform at high levels. The INTASC Standards are "model" standards and intended to be a RESOURCE that all states can use to develop their own state standards. INTASC's hope is that states will agree with and hone the values in the model standards, and in this way move toward consensus and compatible educational policies around what good teaching looks like and how it can be assessed.

Special thanks to the Council of Chief State School Officers for permission to use the INTASC Standards in *Ready for Anything: Supporting New Teachers for Success.*

Standard 1: Content Pedagogy

The teacher understands the central concepts, tools of inquiry, and structures of the discipline he or she teaches and can create learning experiences that make these aspects of subject matter meaningful for students.

1.1 demonstrates an understanding of the central concepts of his or her discipline

1.2 uses explanations and representations that link curriculum to prior learning

1.3 evaluates resources and curriculum materials for appropriateness to the curriculum instructional delivery

1.4 engages students in interpreting ideas from a variety of perspectives

1.5 uses interdisciplinary approaches to teaching and learning

1.6 uses methods of inquiry that are central to the discipline

Standard 2: Student Development

The teacher understands how children learn and develop, and can provide learning opportunities that support a child's intellectual, social, and personal development.

2.1 evaluates student performance to design instructional approaches for social, cognitive, and emotional development

2.2 creates relevance for students by linking with their prior experiences

(continues)

INTASC Standards
(Continued)

2.3 provides opportunities for students to assume responsibility for and be actively engaged in their learning

2.4 encourages student reflection on prior knowledge and its connection to new information

2.5 assesses student thinking as a basis for instructional activities through group/individual interaction and written work (listening, encouraging discussion, eliciting samples of student thinking orally and in writing)

Standard 3: Diverse Learners

The teacher understands how students differ in their approaches to learning and creates instructional opportunities that are adapted to diverse learners.

3.1 designs instruction appropriate to students' stages of development, learning styles, strengths, and needs

3.2 selects approaches that provide opportunities for different performance models

3.3 accesses appropriate services or resources to meet exceptional learning needs

3.4 adjusts instruction to accommodate the learning differences or needs of students (time and circumstance of work, tasks assigned, communication and response modes)

3.5 uses knowledge of different cultural contexts within the community (socio-economic, ethnic, cultural) and connects with the learner through types of interaction and assignments

3.6 creates a learning community that respects individual differences

Standard 4: Multiple Instructional Strategies

The teacher understands and uses a variety of instructional strategies to encourage student development of critical thinking, problem solving, and performance skills.

4.1 selects and uses multiple teaching and learning strategies (a variety of presentations/explanations) to encourage students in critical thinking and problem solving

4.2 encourages students to assume responsibility for identifying and using learning resources

Standard 5: Motivation and Management

The teacher uses an understanding of individual and group motivation and behavior to create a learning environment that encourages positive social interaction, active engagement in learning, and self-motivation.

5.1 encourages clear procedures and expectations that ensure students assume responsibility for themselves and others, work collaboratively and independently, and engage in purposeful learning activities

5.2 engages students by relating lessons to students' personal interests, allowing students to have choices in their learning, and leading students to ask questions and solve problems that are meaningful to them

5.3 organizes, allocates, and manages time, space, and activities in a way that is conducive to learning

5.4 organizes, prepares students for, and monitors independent and group work that allows for full and varied participation of all individuals

INTASC Standards
(Continued)

5.5 analyzes classroom environment and interactions and makes adjustments to enhance social relationships, student motivation/engagement, and productive work

Standard 6: Communication and Technology

The teacher uses knowledge of effective verbal, nonverbal, and media communication techniques to foster active inquiry, collaboration, and supportive interaction in the classroom.

6.1 models effective communication strategies in conveying ideas and information and when asking questions (e.g., monitoring the effects of messages, restating ideas, and drawing connections; using visual, aural, and kinesthetic cues; being sensitive to nonverbal cues both given and received)

6.2 provides support for learner expression in speaking, writing, and other media

6.3 demonstrates that communication is sensitive to gender and cultural differences (e.g., appropriate use of eye contact, interpretation of body language and verbal statements, acknowledgment of and responsiveness to difference modes of communication and participation)

6.4 uses a variety of media communication tools to enrich learning opportunities

Standard 7: Planning

The teacher plans instruction based upon knowledge of subject matter, students, the community, and curriculum goals.

7.1 plans lessons and activities to address variation in learning styles and performance modes, multiple development levels

of diverse learners, and problem solving and exploration

7.2 develops plans that are appropriate for curriculum goals and are based on effective instruction

7.3 adjusts plans to respond to unanticipated sources of input and/or student needs

Standard 8: Assessment

The teacher understands and uses formal and informal assessment strategies to evaluate and ensure the continuous intellectual, social, and physical development of the learner.

8.1 selects, constructs, and uses assessment strategies appropriate to the learning outcomes

8.2 uses a variety of informal and formal strategies to inform choices about student progress and to adjust instruction (e.g., standardized test data, peer and student self-assessment, informal assessments such as observations, surveys, interviews, student work, performance tasks, portfolio, and teacher-made tests)

8.3 uses assessment strategies to involve learners in self-assessment activities to help them become aware of their strengths and needs, and to encourage them to set personal goals for learning

8.4 evaluates the effects of class activities on individuals and on groups through observation of classroom interaction, questioning, and analysis of student work

8.5 maintains useful records of student work and performance and can communicate student progress knowledgeably and responsibly

(continues)

INTASC Standards

(Continued)

8.6 solicits information about students' experiences, learning behavior, needs, and progress from parents, other colleagues, and students

Standard 9: Reflective Practice: Professional Development

The teacher is a reflective practitioner who continually evaluates the effects of his or her choices and actions on others and who actively seeks out opportunities to grow professionally.

9.1 uses classroom observation, information about students, and research as sources for evaluating the outcomes of teaching and learning and as a basis for experimenting with, reflecting on, and revising practice

9.2 uses professional literature, colleagues, and other resources to support self-development as a learner and as a teacher

9.3 consults with professional colleagues within the school and other professional arenas as support for reflection, problem solving, and new ideas, actively sharing experiences and seeking and giving feedback

Standard 10: School and Community Involvement

The teacher fosters relationships with school colleagues, parents, and agencies in the larger community to support students' learning and well-being.

10.1 participates in collegial activities designed to make the entire school a productive learning environment

10.2 links with counselors, teachers of other classes and activities within the school, professionals in community agencies, and others in the community to support students' learning and well-being

10.3 seeks to establish cooperative partnerships with parents/guardians to support student learning

10.4 advocates for students

Seminar Planner

	Seminar Topic	Seminar Focus	Date and Time
Seminar 1	Beginning the Teaching Profession	■ INTASC Standards 1–10 ■ The logistics of teaching ■ Beginning organization ■ Beginning management ■ Beginning the first day and the first week of school	
Seminar 2	Classroom Atmosphere	■ INTASC Standard 6 ■ Creating a welcoming and efficient classroom	
Seminar 3	Classroom Management	■ INTASC Standard 5 ■ Organization and management of students, time, and workload	
Seminar 4	Strategic Planning and Lesson Design	■ INTASC Standard 7 ■ Effective planning and lesson design	
Seminar 5	The Engaging Classroom	■ INTASC Standard 4 ■ Strategies to actively engage all students in learning	
Seminar 6	Observations and Evaluations	■ INTASC Standards 1–10 ■ Indicators of effective performance	
Seminar 7	Stress Management	■ INTASC Standard 9 ■ Managing time, work, and your life	
Seminar 8	Effective Questioning	■ INTASC Standard 4 ■ Questioning strategies and techniques	
Seminar 9	The Test	■ INTASC Standard 8 ■ Helping students with state testing	
Seminar 10	Surviving the Last Weeks of School	■ INTASC Standard 10 ■ Organization for the end of the school year ■ Ending the last week with students	
Seminar 11	Success and Celebrations	■ Reflecting on the year ■ Celebrating with students and peers	

Seminar Planning Checklist

Task	Completed
❏ Print invitation and seminar overview	
❏ Deliver invitation to participants (one week before seminar)	
❏ Post seminar overview in teacher's workroom (for teachers other than invitees who might want to attend)	
Print, collate, and hole-punch all participant handouts (one set per person): ❏ Seminar overview page	
❏ Seminar strategies pages and reproducibles	
❏ Seminar reflections page	
❏ Seminar "I'm Ready for Anything" Self-Assessment	
Gather materials and supplies for: ❏ Facilitator strategies (see individual seminars)	
❏ Teacher-directed student activities (see individual seminars)	
❏ Arrange for refreshments	
❏ Arrange for audiovisual equipment	
❏ Get door prizes	
❏ Reproduce Special Request forms	
❏ Coordinate guest speakers	
❏ Set up classroom visitation schedule	
❏ Set conferencing schedule	

Special Request Form

Special Request

Name of teacher

Room number

Special request

Time of day preferred

Special Request

Name of teacher

Room number

Special request

Time of day preferred

Seminar (1) Beginning the Teaching Profession

Contents

CATHERINE DID NOT START OUT as an exemplary teacher. She entered the education profession as a lateral entry with no formal training or coursework. Her degree was in French and religion; her assignment was reading and one class each of introductory French and Spanish. When Catherine called me for help, I realized that, as a veteran, I had forgotten the stress of day-to-day teaching and the challenges of a diverse student population. Working with a first-year teacher was difficult, and demanded extreme effort and patience from both of us. Catherine was determined to be the best teacher in the world, but it became obvious from her questions that she had no clue what to expect from the first day.

We spent a year together, planning and designing "what works for Catherine" and the best instructional practices for her students. Weekends were dedicated to lesson plans, discipline issues, and conflicts with administration and parents. Our work together necessitated a careful balance between her enthusiastic naïveté and my long years of experience. I saw the passion and commitment that she brought to her job and we constantly laughed at my favorite phrase: *"Do not quit."*

This experience awoke in me a special passion for new teachers. I will always remember one of Catherine's comments to me during that first year: "I want to be just like you. You were the best seventh-grade teacher anyone could ever have." That year, a long time ago, started a wonderful relationship with a former student who is now a colleague and friend.

Introduction

Goal To provide tips, ideas, suggestions, and logistical support for the first weeks of school

Time frame One day

Agenda

Welcome to the World of Teaching

Schedule and Seminar Details

Seminar 1: Beginning the Teaching Profession

Facilitator Strategies: The Logistics of Teaching

Facilitator Strategies: Beginning Organization

Facilitator Strategies: Beginning Management

Teacher-Directed Student Activities: Beginning the First Day and Week

Seminar 1 Reflections

"I'm Ready for Anything" Self-Assessment

WELCOME TO THE WORLD OF TEACHING!

This fulfilling, rewarding career enables you to touch the lives of hundreds of children. The first year of teaching will be full of challenges, and it will be very difficult. No one has a foolproof prescription for becoming an effective teacher, and there are always new ideas and strategies to try. *Ready for Anything: Supporting New Teachers for Success* is a process that develops the skills and knowledge that new teachers need to assist and improve student achievement and growth. It is full of strategies and activities, passion, and commitment, and will greatly enhance your potential to become a qualified educator. It is the beginning of a wonderful experience that all new teachers should have, with full support and guidance.

Overview

Seminar 1 is about the successful start of a new career in teaching. It is about knowing what to do during the first days of school, the logistics of opening school, creating an atmosphere, and beginning management for the first weeks with the students. This one-day, welcoming workshop is designed to help new teachers get to know the school and each other. It gives participants time to share refreshments and discussions, opportunities to hear stories about school success, and a chance to feel the excitement and energy that new teachers bring to a school. It allows time to make new staff comfortable with the building, other personnel, and policies and procedures, and guides participation in strategies and activities for use with students during the first two weeks of school. Individual school policies and expectations should be an integral component of Seminar 1, which is designed by the new-teacher executive committee and includes site-based information for the staff.

Structure

This first seminar has four sections, beginning with introductions and a scavenger hunt. It then discusses organizational tools, offers a few management strategies, and ends with activities to use with students during the first several weeks. Numerous facilitator-directed strategies provide the skills and knowledge the new teacher needs to open school. In addition, the facilitator models teacher-directed student activities and use of the reproducibles, so that teachers can use these activities on the first day with students. Time for socializing and interaction are built into the seminar, as are opportunities for discussion and questions.

Preparation

Materials New-teacher binder, lesson plan notebook, bucket of fun, reproducibles (*figures 1.4–1.19*), district acronyms, staff handbook, paper, markers, construction paper, miscellaneous audiovisual equipment, sample gradebook, index cards, craft sticks (optional), refreshments, door prizes, Special Request form

TODAY'S SEMINAR FOCUSES on logistics, planning, expectations, and student activities for the first weeks of school. Begin by sending an invitation and seminar overview to all new teachers at least one week before the meeting date. Gather items for the Bucket of Fun (*see figure 1.3*) and make copies of the reproducibles for distribution to seminar participants. You will need copies of the following:

- Invitation (*figure 1.1*)
- Seminar 1 Overview (*figure 1.2*)
- INTASC Standards 1–10 (*figure A*)
- New-Teacher Bucket of Fun label (*figure 1.3*)
- Reproducibles for facilitator strategies and teacher-directed student activities (*figures 1.4–1.17*)
- Seminar 1 Reflections (*figure 1.18*)
- "I'm Ready for Anything" Self-Assessment (*figure 1.19*)
- Special Request form (*figure D*)

Tip

Take time to share refreshments, have discussions, trade your stories of success, and build excitement and energy. Be sure to familiarize new staff with the school building, other personnel, and policies and procedures. The energy level will be high, but don't overwhelm beginning staff members with too much information. Remember, the *Ready for Anything* program is about step-by-step strategies, appropriately spaced over time and always modeled.

Tip

Have a wonderful selection
of food and snacks for the first
seminar.

Facilitator Strategies: The Logistics of Teaching

Focus Getting to know the school and what is expected before
and during the school year.

How to Use This section is about exploring the school and
becoming familiar with the staff, the building, and the rules and
procedures that apply to all personnel. The strategies in this
section are designed to provide a background for state, district,
and school daily operations and key functions.

Welcome to Your New Home

A tic-tac-toe-type game, done as a group activity, is used to introduce new staff members to the area. Create 16 questions related
to your state and area to place in the grid. Award prizes for the
most correct answers. *See figure 1.4.*

Your School Scavenger Hunt

Give teams of new teachers questions that can be answered by
touring the school. (The number of members on a team will depend
on the number of participants.) Award prizes to the team with the
most correct answers. *See figure 1.5.*

The ABCs of the System

Review the names and acronyms of the many programs in your
school and district. Be sure to include those that are specific to
your district. *See figure 1.6.*

Who, What, When, Where, and How

Hold a meet-and-greet session to introduce key school personnel
to the new staff. Share a list of nonnegotiable matters in school
and district policies and procedures.

Looks Are Everything!

Brainstorm a list of do's and don'ts in regard to appropriate,
professional dress. Review the dress code(s) for your district and
your specific school.

Getting It All Together

Provide a copy of the staff handbook for review of the procedures
that could affect the first day. Save the rest of the handbook for
later.

Facilitator Strategies: Beginning Organization

Focus How to organize the classroom, paperwork, equipment, and daily lessons.

How to Use This section is about how to effectively manage all the paperwork and forms that are required by the school. The strategies in this section are designed to provide a series of organizational tools, modeled by the facilitator, that help with planning, materials, classroom arrangement, audiovisual equipment, displays, and grading.

The New-Teacher Binder

For each participant, provide a large, three-ring binder with tabs for each seminar. Label the front with the participant's name and *"Ready for Anything: Supporting New Teachers for Success."* Place a copy of INTASC Standards 1–10 in each binder; you will be discussing these with seminar participants throughout the year. Make sure participants bring their binders to each seminar during the year, to collect strategies and activities.

INTASC Standards

The INTASC Standards (*see figure A*) are designed to be a resource for guiding effective instructional practices. An effective teacher must be able to integrate content knowledge with the specific strengths and needs of students to ensure that all students learn and perform at high levels. Provide a copy of the standards in each new-teacher binder; take time to review them and discuss the importance of each strand. During each seminar, take time to discuss the pertinent standard and related competencies, as they are integrated as an instructional focus point on what effective teachers should know and be able to do. (Seminar 6 provides an extensive discussion of the standards, along with observation and evaluation.)

Lesson Plan Notebook

Help new teachers gather the components of a lesson plan notebook, including the school's lesson design template. Have examples of exemplary lesson plans on hand for new staff to use as models. You may also want to include tabs for parent contacts, discipline logs, and additional materials.

Tip

Help new teachers understand that no classroom procedure is too insignificant to practice—and practice repeatedly. It is the consistent implementation of logistical procedures that will help ensure a successful year.

Special Request Form

Provide a copy of the Special Request form (*see figure D*) at each seminar. This facilitator communication tool is a request for additional support and guidance, and should be used whenever the new teacher feels it necessary, at any time of the year.

Materials and Supplies

Using the reproducible checklist, collect the materials and supplies for the first week of school. *See figure 1.7.*

Arranging the Room

Discuss ideas and suggestions for making the most of movement patterns and seating arrangements for the classroom. Visit each classroom and share ideas for the optimal seating and space arrangement.

The Focus Board

Create focus signs or placards for the front board, such as: Objective, Warm-Up, Essential Questions, Date, Agenda, Homework.

Working with Audiovisual Equipment

Give time for new teachers to practice the use and operation of audiovisual equipment, including: overhead projectors (and bulb changes therefor), VCRs and TVs, computer projector devices, copy machines, fax machine, laminator.

Classroom Displays

Discuss inexpensive ideas for creating bulletin boards, wall-space displays, word walls, Star Student Work areas, and other visual displays.

Gradebook Review

Have new teachers list the essential components of a gradebook, including grades, absences, and tardy codes. Review the grading scale and the school grading policies.

Facilitator Strategies: Beginning Management

Focus Simple management strategies to use on a daily basis.

How to Use This section provides new teachers with simple, easy-to-implement behavior management strategies, all of which are designed to help teachers establish procedures and learn how to effectively manage a classroom. It is only a small sampling of the numerous behavior management techniques available, and the facilitator should remain flexible about using prior knowledge and experience to share and implement additional strategies. Classroom management is the most urgent topic; questions and concerns about student behavior will be asked at every seminar. Take time to discuss ideas and solutions. New teachers should also be made aware that if severe problems occur, they should contact the administration immediately for support and help. You cannot overemphasize the importance of clear and consistent management processes, step-by-step directions, and building positive relationships with students.

Establishing Procedures

The most important component of new-teacher support is immediate establishment of procedures for smooth classroom operation. Emphasize how critical it is to have procedures firmly in place, repeated consistently, and modeled for students. Visit each classroom regularly to provide feedback on the effectiveness of the teacher's implementation. *See figure 1.8.*

Teacher Readiness Survey

Discuss the operational components of an effective classroom using the Teacher Readiness Survey (*figure 1.9*). Use this template as a guide for providing feedback during classroom visits.

The Spot

Decide on a location in the room where the teacher will be whenever he or she gives directions, so that student attention will be focused consistently. Place a small X on the spot where the teacher should stand when giving instructions.

Tip

Teachers should not announce to every student that they are first-day (-year) teachers. If they are nervous, encourage them to go ahead and be nervous on the inside, but let the outside portray organization and readiness. In other words, fake it!

Tip

The teacher should explain to students what he or she will do, what they will do, how the teacher will monitor what they do, and what will happen when they don't do what the teacher wants.

Proximity

Model for new staff how to walk over and stand close to a student. Remind teachers not to stop talking while they do this; the idea is to let the student know nonverbally that the teacher is aware of the student's behavior.

Six-Step Directions

Share with and model the six-step direction process for new teachers. It is important for new staff to understand that simple, step-by-step directions will guide students through the work process in a consistent and organized manner. Emphasize the "See it, Say it, and Write it" model as teachers give directions to students (to accommodate multiple learning styles). Make sure that there are visual, written directions for students to see. Use these steps when giving oral directions: *when, who, what, ask, time, action*. An example of this process is:

- WHEN—"In one minute . . ."
- WHO—"Everyone in the class . . ."
- WHAT—"Will complete a learning log . . ."
- ASK—"What questions do you have . . . ?"
- ACTION—"You may begin . . ."; "Get started . . ."
- TIME—"You have five minutes to finish . . ."

Positive Phone Call

Decide on a set of classroom procedures. To model the activity, write each procedure on a card and put the cards in a bowl. Write student names on another set of cards or on craft sticks. At random, pull out a card and the name of a student. If that student followed the procedure during a set amount of time, call home with the good news.

Calling on All

To model this activity, you will need one deck of cards or a set of craft sticks per participant. Write each student's name on a card or craft stick. Shuffle and proceed through the deck or sticks calling names at random and asking questions of the person chosen.

Positive Repetition

Model the steps of this strategy:

1. Give a direction.
2. Look for a student who is following the direction.
3. Say the student's name, what direction he or she is following, and "thank you."

Circulating

Model the strategy of consistently walking around the classroom. Show how to nonverbally communicate to students that you are recognizing appropriate behavior. Use a stamp/sticker or incentive program, if desired.

Teacher-Directed Student Activities: Beginning the First Day and Week

Focus Welcoming students and setting high expectations for success.

How to Use This section provides new teachers with classroom activities that can be used during the first few days of school. The activities, which should be modeled and explained, are designed to allow students to become familiar with the teacher, the classroom, the school resources, and each other. New teachers need to be reminded that the first few days should be heavily planned, with multiple activities, in addition to those required by the school. These strategies are often used when there is some time left at the end of the teaching block. Make sure that teachers have photocopies of these activities for student use before school starts—just in case!

Meet the Teacher

This activity allows students to get to know you as a teacher. Create 20 multiple-choice questions about yourself. Ask each question and have students discuss possible answers. Give the correct answer and explain why. Sample questions could include: Where was I born? Where did I go to college? What is my favorite food? What is my favorite TV show?

The ABCs of Content

This opening discussion asks students to brainstorm words related to the content. A grid, with a cell for each letter, is used as a template for recording words. Create a vocabulary map graphic organizer to use as a classroom display of key terms and words related to the unit or topic. *See figure 1.10.*

Classroom Scavenger Hunt

The Classroom Scavenger Hunt allows time for students to explore the room. Group students into pairs and give each pair a scavenger hunt worksheet (*figure 1.11*). Allow students 10 minutes to investigate the classroom and fill in the blanks. Award prizes to the top three student pairs.

Tip

Make sure that your new teachers have overplanned for the first few days of schools. The teacher-directed student activities are designed to supplement the beginning of school lesson plans and are intended to build relationships and positive interactions in the classroom.

Textbook Safari

Have students work alone or in pairs to locate answers within a textbook. Review and discuss the importance of understanding the book format, as well as the content, and being able to find information within its pages. *See figure 1.12.*

The Journal Today

"The Journal Today" *(figure 1.13)* is used to focus attention on key material presented during a unit or topic:

- The main idea (explain what you learned about the unit)
- Vocabulary (what key terms and phrases are necessary to understand the content)
- Teacher-generated thinking questions, at various levels, for review (based on Bloom's or Marzano's taxonomies)
- Visual understanding (student-created graphic organizer that illustrates their learning)
- 3–2–1 summary (three things you learned, two questions you have, and one way you will remember the information)

Individual copies of the journal reproducible may be made for students, or students can copy the reproducible format into their notebooks.

It's All About ME!

Get to know your students by using the "It's All About ME!" reproducible *(figure 1.14)*. Allow students time to complete the questionnaire; then share with the class their unique learning styles and modes of understanding. Use these answers later in the year for grouping students by interest and study habits.

Who's Who in the Classroom

Use the "Who's Who in the Classroom" reproducible *(figure 1.15)* and allow time for students to get the signature of the classmates who answer the statement in each grid. Take time to share the information during class.

Tip

Tell your new teachers to take time to get to know their students. Remind them that students like to hear their names pronounced correctly. Ask very young new teachers to become comfortable being called "Mr." or "Ms."; for many, this will be the first time they have been addressed so formally.

Fact or Fiction?

Choose a topic or content area. Create sets of four statements about this area. One of the statements must be false. Read the statements aloud and allow time for thinking and processing. You can use this strategy as a fun way to introduce yourself to the class, and/or have students create statements about themselves to share. If the activity is based on a text, do it before reading the text selection; then have students find proof in the text as to which of the four statements is incorrect. Read the text to check and validate the answers.

Going Around in Circles

Have students use the circles reproducible (*figure 1.16*) to create illustrations incorporating the circles into representations of your chosen content (e.g., history), topic (e.g., frogs), or theme (e.g., relationships). Share the illustrations with the class and display them around the room.

Learning Coupon

Some teachers use a coupon as a motivational tool. Make multiple copies of the learning coupon (*figure 1.17*) for use with your students. Determine the rules and/or procedures for earning a coupon, such as being on time, having materials, or working well collaboratively. Decide how the coupons will be used by the recipients as a special incentive in class (extra test points, line up first, special helper, positive note to take home).

Seminar 1 Reflections

Activity: Expectations for Success

Create a set of words and phrases related to this first seminar by writing each word or phrase on an individual index card. Pass the card sets around the room as a review of the workshop and share comments and questions. *See figure 1.18.*

"I'm Ready for Anything" Self-Assessment (Seminar 1)

See figure 1.19.

Tip

Be on time—for everything. Turn in paperwork, attend staff meetings, and carry out and follow up on your required duties and responsibilities in a timely manner. Establish a reputation as a team player, someone who can be trusted and counted on to follow through with assignments and requests.

You Are Invited!

Seminar 1: Beginning the Teaching Profession

Help Has Arrived for New Teachers!

Date
_____

Time
_____

Location
_____

Information ▪ Ideas ▪ Classroom Survival ▪ Door Prizes
Refreshments ▪ New Friends ▪ Getting Started as a Teacher

Reflections
_____

Are you ready to be a teacher?

What do you expect from your first year of teaching?

Overview

Seminar 1: Beginning the Teaching Profession

Goal

To provide tips, ideas, suggestions, and logistical support for the first weeks of school.

Focus

Today's seminar focuses on logistics, planning, expectations, and strategies for the first weeks of school. Strategies are divided into four categories: the teaching profession, beginning organization, beginning management, and beginning the first week.

Agenda

Welcome to the World of Teaching

Schedule and Seminar Details

Seminar 1: Beginning the Teaching Profession

- Facilitator Strategies: The Logistics of Teaching
  - ☐ Welcome to Your New Home
  - ☐ Your School Scavenger Hunt
  - ☐ The ABCs of the District
  - ☐ Who, What, When, Where, and How
  - ☐ Looks Are Everything!
  - ☐ Getting It All Together

- Facilitator Strategies: Beginning Organization
  - ☐ The New-Teacher Binder
  - ☐ INTASC Standards
  - ☐ Lesson Plan Notebook
  - ☐ Special Request Form
  - ☐ Materials and Supplies

Agenda (Continued)

  - ☐ Arranging the Room
  - ☐ The Focus Board
  - ☐ Working with Audiovisual Equipment
  - ☐ Classroom Displays
  - ☐ Gradebook Review

- Facilitator Strategies: Beginning Management
  - ☐ Establishing Procedures
  - ☐ Teacher Readiness Survey
  - ☐ The Spot
  - ☐ Proximity
  - ☐ Six-Step Directions
  - ☐ Positive Phone Call
  - ☐ Calling on All
  - ☐ Positive Repetition
  - ☐ Circulating

- Teacher-Directed Student Activities: Beginning the First Day and Week
  - ☐ Meet the Teacher
  - ☐ The ABCs of Content
  - ☐ Classroom Scavenger Hunt
  - ☐ Textbook Safari
  - ☐ The Journal Today
  - ☐ It's All About ME!
  - ☐ Who's Who in the Classroom
  - ☐ Fact or Fiction?
  - ☐ Going Around in Circles
  - ☐ Learning Coupon

Seminar 1 Reflections

"I'm Ready for Anything" Self-Assessment

New-Teacher Bucket of Fun

Collect the following assortment of teacher-related items (or similar items) and place them in a bucket or bag that has an attached label with a graphic of a beach bucket.

Water is for your health

Crayon is to color your day

Marble is to replace the ones you will lose

Lifesaver is for the support program

Peanuts are so you can get a little nutty

Tissue is for the tears of joy

Lip balm is for too much talking

Payday candy bar is for the first check

Band-Aids are for all the little mistakes

Overhead marker pens are for sharing your thoughts

Welcome to Your New Home

State capitol	County in which school is located	Name of the city or town mayor	State bird
Three points of interest in the state	A sports team	Number of counties in the state	Name of a local paper
Nickname for the state	Closest shopping mall	Anyone famous born in the state	Largest city in the state
National park, forest, or other "wild" area in the state	Bordering states	Name of the state governor	Three major industries in the state or area

Your School Scavenger Hunt

name of the school

_____

school main telephone number

_____

school mascot

_____

price of an adult lunch

_____

teacher work times

_____

location of the copy machine

_____

name of a secretary

_____

name of your hall's custodian

_____

the mission statement for the school

_____

school colors

_____

location of the closest telephone

_____

cost of a soda and snack

_____

school courier number

_____

the first day for student attendance

_____

how many days you get for winter break

_____

three steps to take when a lockdown is called

_____

_____

name of the principal

_____

who or how to call for a substitute

_____

two items of clothing you are not allowed to wear

_____

location of the closest restroom

_____

person who will get you classroom supplies

_____

number of staff mailboxes

_____

the college the principal graduated from

_____

one item hanging in the entrance to the school

_____

three things found in the teacher's work area

_____

_____

names of three office staff members working today

_____

_____

The ABCs of the System

ADD	attention deficit disorder		**INTASC**	Interstate New Teacher Assessment and Support Consortium
ADHD	attention deficit disorder with hyperactivity		**IPT**	language proficiency test
ADM	average daily membership		**LD**	learning disabled
AL	annual leave		**LEA**	local education agency
AP	advanced placement assistant principal		**LEP**	limited English proficient
AV	audiovisual		**NAEP**	National Assessment of Educational Programs
AVID	advancement via individual determination		**NBPTS**	National Board for Professional Teaching Standards
AYP	annual yearly progress		**NCLB**	No Child Left Behind
BEH	behaviorally/emotionally handicapped		**NEA**	National Education Association
BOE	Board of Education		**OH**	orthopedically handicapped
CEU	continuing education units		**OHI**	other health impaired
DEP	differentiated education plan		**PBL**	problem-based learning
DPI	Department of Public Instruction		**PEP**	personalized education plans
EC	exceptional children		**PTSA**	Parent Teacher Student Association
ELL	English language learners		**SIP**	school improvement plan
EMH	educable mentally handicapped		**SL**	sick leave
ESL	English as a Second Language		**SLT**	school leadership team
F & R	free and reduced[-price] lunch		**TA**	teacher assistant
HR	human resources		**TIMSS**	Third International Math and Science Study
IB	international baccalaureate		**TMH**	trainable mentally handicapped
IDEA	Individuals with Disabilities Education Act			
IEP	individual education program			

Materials and Supplies Checklist

For Your Desk

- ❑ gradebook
- ❑ lesson plan book
- ❑ substitute's folder
- ❑ overhead marker pens
- ❑ scissors
- ❑ stapler and staples
- ❑ paper clips
- ❑ hole punch
- ❑ tape
- ❑ index cards
- ❑ textbooks (teacher editions)
- ❑ calculator
- ❑ toiletry kit
- ❑ plastic bandage strips
- ❑ change for vending machine
- ❑ safety pins
- ❑ timer
- ❑ small set of tools
- ❑ chalk or dry-erase markers
- ❑ rubber bands
- ❑ pencils, pens

For Your Classroom

- ❑ pencils, crayons, markers
- ❑ rulers
- ❑ glue and tape
- ❑ overhead projector
- ❑ writing paper
- ❑ tissues
- ❑ bulletin board trims
- ❑ calendar
- ❑ art supplies
- ❑ plants (optional)
- ❑ dictionaries
- ❑ focus board signs
- ❑ storage tubs
- ❑ _____
- ❑ _____
- ❑ _____
- ❑ _____
- ❑ _____
- ❑ _____
- ❑ _____
- ❑ _____

Establishing Procedures

☐ entering the classroom _____

☐ exiting the classroom _____

☐ lining up to go to another area _____

☐ moving through the halls _____

☐ getting ready for the start of class _____

☐ listening to the teacher's directions _____

☐ sharpening pencils _____

☐ getting supplies _____

☐ going to the restroom during class _____

☐ passing out papers or materials _____

☐ turning in homework _____

☐ getting the teacher's attention _____

☐ fire drills, crisis drills, lockdowns _____

☐ working individually _____

☐ working with a partner or group _____

☐ using classroom computer(s) _____

☐ test-taking procedures _____

☐ taking notes and getting the notebook ready _____

☐ getting ready to leave class _____

Teacher Readiness Survey

Observable Behaviors	Monday	Tuesday	Wednesday	Thursday	Friday
Students entering/exiting the room					
Warm-up and Daily Objective posted					
Essential Questions posted					
Homework posted					
Attendance completed					
Tardies					
Discipline plan posted • Rules, rewards, consequences					
Hall pass or agenda					
Classroom atmosphere: • Bulletin boards • Front board • Word wall • Entrance to room • Student work					
Desk arrangement					
Materials ready					
Homework returned/graded					
Lesson design • Lesson plans current/visible					

The ABCs of Content

A	B	C	D	E	F
G	H	I	J	K	L
M	N	O	P	Q	R
S	T	U	V	W	X
Y	Z				

Name

Date

Classroom Scavenger Hunt

number of desks . . . . _____

brand of pencil sharpener . . . . _____

number of drawers in the room . . . . _____

classroom door number . . . . _____

color(s) of the textbook(s) . . . . _____

location of the Daily Objective . . . . _____

brand of television . . . . _____

location of posted homework . . . . _____

place(s) where students may put bookbags . . . . _____

location of make-up work folder . . . . _____

color of front board . . . . _____

number of light bulbs in the room . . . . _____

location of hall pass . . . . _____

number of windows . . . . _____

teacher's name . . . . _____

number of students . . . . _____

brand of clock . . . . _____

Name _____

Date _____

Textbook Safari

name of textbook . . . . _____

name of the textbook publisher . . . . _____

location of the glossary . . . . _____

title of the first chapter . . . . _____

page numbers in the index . . . . _____

title of chapter 3 . . . . _____

a page with a graph or map . . . . _____

three pages with pictures, and the titles of the pictures . . . . _____

_____

_____

_____

copyright date . . . . _____

name of a famous person in the book (if applicable) . . . . _____

three bold-faced words and the page numbers
on which they appear . . . . _____

_____

_____

name of the textbook author(s) . . . . _____

place the book was published . . . . _____

last word in the glossary . . . . _____

first entry in the index . . . . _____

number of pages in the book . . . . _____

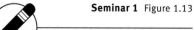

Name

Date

The Journal Today

The Journal Today	*Focus for the Day*
MAIN IDEA	

Vocabulary	Q U E S T I O N I N G
Words of the Day	1.
Suffixes	2.
Prefixes	3.
Root Words	4.
	5.
	6.

3 **2** **1**	**Graphic Organizer**

It's All About ME!

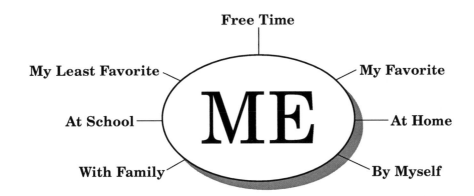

My preference about music when I study is . . . . . music on   music off

My preference on an assignment is . . . . alone   with a partner

I like to work . . . . on the floor   at a table   in a comfortable chair

Usually if I forget an assignment, it's because . . . it's boring   I need help   I'm busy

I am more alert . . . . in the morning   at lunch   in the evening

I like to sit in class . . . . in the front   in the middle   in the back

I like to be near . . . . the door   a window   a wall   my friends

If I have something to do . . . . I read directions   I start quickly   I don't start

If something is new . . . . I want it explained   I want to figure it out myself

I like to . . . . read   write   draw   make things

I like a room to be . . . . brightly lit   dimly lit

When working, I like to . . . . drink liquids   eat and snack   neither

I am good at finishing things . . . . yes   no

Name _____

Date _____

Who's Who in the Classroom

Likes pizza	Has a 5 in the home phone number	Has been to the beach	Likes vanilla ice cream	Has a dog
Born in April	Has been to a play	Has a brother or sister	Has been on a plane	Has been fishing
Likes to roller-blade	Has run a race	**ME**	Favorite color is green	Likes to read about sports
Likes to sing	Born out of state	Likes apples	Likes to chew gum	Likes to go camping
Has been to a scary movie	Likes football	Is left-handed	Has been to a theme park	Likes video games

Going Around in Circles

Name

Date

Name _____

Date _____

Learning Coupon

HOMEWORK COUPON

Name _____

To be used by [date] _____

Teacher _____

How to use the coupon _____

_____

HOMEWORK COUPON

Name _____

To be used by [date] _____

Teacher _____

How to use the coupon _____

_____

HOMEWORK COUPON

Name _____

To be used by [date] _____

Teacher _____

How to use the coupon _____

_____

HOMEWORK COUPON

Name _____

To be used by [date] _____

Teacher _____

How to use the coupon _____

_____

HOMEWORK COUPON

Name _____

To be used by [date] _____

Teacher _____

How to use the coupon _____

_____

HOMEWORK COUPON

Name _____

To be used by [date] _____

Teacher _____

How to use the coupon _____

_____

Seminar 1 Reflections

Activity: Expectations for Success

Create a set of words and phrases related to this first seminar by writing each word or phrase on an individual index card. Pass the card sets around the room as a review of the workshop and share comments and questions.

Suggested terms include: *your new state, your new school, acronyms, audiovisual equipment, dress code, classroom displays, paperwork, lesson plans, classroom management, beginning activities, procedures and rules, support and help.*

Self-Assessment

"I'm Ready for Anything" Self-Assessment (Seminar 1)

How Am I Doing?	Personal Comments
Have I toured the school and found the materials, restrooms, offices, copy machine, drink and snack machines?	
Have I attended the Ready for Anything: Supporting New Teachers for Success *opening workshop (Seminar 1)?*	
Have I collected my classroom supplies?	
Have I met with the principal, the grade-level chair, and my mentor?	
Do I know who to contact for help with . . . ?	
Have I reviewed the staff handbook for drills and crisis plans?	
Have I organized the procedures for teaching the first day and the first week?	
Do I have my class rosters, insurance forms, receipt book, calculator, and so on ready for the first day?	
Have I organized my week with beginning activities?	
Have I selected and organized the strategies for the first week? Have I printed the student handouts?	
Have I completed the first-day planning checklist?	
AM I READY TO START?	

Seminar ② Classroom Atmosphere

Contents

THERE COMES A TIME IN EVERY TEACHER'S
life when you know you have the best classroom in the school.
Not only is it the most decorated and the most often photo-
graphed, but other teachers and visitors also frequent your
class to get an understanding of the importance of atmosphere,
through the welcoming warmth and coziness of the room.

Every day for about six months, MO would come to visit.
He was very pleasant and never, ever disturbed the students.
The children would watch MO move about the room, making
observations and pausing to reflect on the quality of the work
being produced. He would venture over to Mr. B's room and do
the same, taking in all he could and analyzing every situation
carefully. Students often spoke to MO and were more than
respectful of the fact that he was quite small, compared to them;
they were apologetic when MO tripped over their feet and bookbags. As the proud teacher, I always had an open-door policy.

One day, though, MO just didn't come back, and we always
wondered what had happened to him. We guessed that the life
span of a mouse was not very long.

Introduction

Goal To provide tips, ideas, suggestions, and activities to enhance the classroom learning environment

Time frame Two hours

Agenda

Welcome Back and Success Stories; Concerns and Questions

Discussion of INTASC Standard 6: Communication and Technology

Seminar 2: Classroom Atmosphere

Facilitator Strategies

Teacher-Directed Student Activities

Seminar 2 Reflections

"I'm Ready for Anything" Self-Assessment

TEACHING IS ABOUT BUILDING RELATIONSHIPS.

Every day I asked myself: "Would I want to be a student in my classroom?" Reflecting on how I responded to my students gave me the opportunity to reevaluate the physical and emotional atmosphere in my room. The moment they walk into a classroom, students know what type of teacher you are. They want to see a neat, colorful classroom filled with items that catch their interest. Posters, lamps, books, stuffed animals, plants, and motivational banners should invite students to enter and be ready to work. It should be evident from the first glance of a classroom that every child is valued and appreciated. A teacher who creates a student-centered, adult-driven classroom has tremendous potential to improve student achievement.

Overview

Classroom atmosphere includes all the things that surround the student: sights, sounds, and smells. Creating an atmosphere that is attractive, functional, and instructionally appropriate is critical to making students feel successful in their work. Student work, bulletin boards, and displays should reflect—and help create— an atmosphere in which risk-taking is acceptable and encouraged, and where mutual respect is the daily norm. Teachers must provide a clear definition of high expectations and model behavior to meet those expectations from the first day. For example, the teacher's voice should reflect authority, but also care and respect.

Preparation

Materials Photographs of exemplary bulletin boards and classroom displays, reproducibles (*figures 2.3–2.12*), classrooms for visitation and observation, refreshments, door prizes, Special Request form

TODAY'S SEMINAR FOCUSES on strategies for creating a positive classroom environment that supports student achievement and helps build relationships. The activities, modeled by the facilitator, are structured so that teachers can connect quickly with students by selecting activities that they feel are most appropriate to their students' grade level. You will need copies of the following:

- Invitation (*figure 2.1*)
- INTASC Standard 6: Communication and Technology (*see figure A*)
- Seminar 2 Overview (*figure 2.2*)
- Reproducibles for facilitator strategies and teacher-directed student activities (*figures 2.3–2.9*)
- Seminar 2 Reflections (*figures 2.10 and 2.11*)
- "I'm Ready for Anything" Self-Assessment (*figure 2.12*)
- Special Request form (*figure D*)

Tip

Use relaxing music when participants first come into the seminar.

Tip

Ask your teachers to reflect on this question daily: "Would you like to be a student in your classroom?"

Facilitator Strategies

Focus Using effective verbal and nonverbal communication, working with transitions, celebrating success.

How to Use Use the following strategies to help new teachers enhance their communication and build relationships with students.

Body Language 101

Model various types of nonverbal communication strategies for teachers to use when working with students. Explain that some teachers get immediate results by "just looking" at a student, whereas others use eye contact, thumbs up, proximity and a smile, and bending down to the student's level.

Transitions with Music

Discuss the importance of music in the classroom. Transitions between activities and independent work time are great places to use appropriate music selections. Talk about how to use music when students enter the classroom as the bell activity (transition) is completed.

New Teacher in the Movies

Be brave and set up a video camera in the back of the classroom. Choose whether you wish to tell the students that you are making the video. In the privacy of your home, watch the tape to identify your interaction patterns with students. Observe how you walk around the room, when you call on students, who you call on, the location where you give directions, how effective those directions are, and other things. Conscious awareness of all these items builds effective teaching practices.

Beginning Bulletin Boards

It seems that teachers either like or don't like bulletin boards. If you use one, decide on the type of displays you want before you set it up. Include some of the following: star student work, current events, humor and quotes in education, content topics, or what's happening at school. Make sure that you change the bulletin board often so that it reflects current topics and units.

Graphic Organizers

Provide a set of graphic organizers for each new teacher. Suggest ideas on how to use each as a bell activity (transition activity), teacher input method, review, test, and independent practice. *See figures 2.3–2.7.*

Teacher-Directed Student Activities

Focus Creating and celebrating student success.

Everyone Has a Story to Tell

Once a week, allow students to reflect on what worked for their learning in the classroom. Take time to explore the "Aha!" moments of student success. Tell personal stories of learning success and tools that you developed to help improve your achievement and overcome learning obstacles.

Three-Second Cheers

Celebrate success every day by using "Three-Second Cheers" (*figure 2.8*) on a random basis in the classroom to recognize simple accomplishments. Select three or four of the Three-Second Cheers to implement in your classroom. Teach each procedure to the students and have fun with some simple motivation! Have students brainstorm additional cheers for use in the room.

Thought of the Day

Each week, post a new quote or saying in the classroom. This provides an excellent writing prompt for students and can be used with any content area. *See figure 2.9.*

Star Student Work

Create an area in the room where student work can be displayed. Decide on a purpose for sharing the work (for example, best writing, creative illustrations, great math-problem solutions). Put up work on a regular basis; include the student's name and a reason why the work is fantastic and a model for others.

Tip

Help teachers understand that the classroom should be an extension of who they are, and should reflect their enthusiasm for and excitement about learning.

Quote

They may forget what you said, but they will never forget how you made them feel.

—Carl W. Buechner

Seminar 2 Reflections

Activity: Classroom Crawl

Beginning teachers will go on a classroom scavenger hunt adventure. Talk about the Classroom Crawl workpage and allow participants time to rate each room and offer suggestions or comments. Have them leave the completed forms on the desk for the classroom teacher's review. *See figures 2.10 and 2.11.*

"I'm Ready for Anything" Self-Assessment (Seminar 2)

See figure 2.12.

You Are Invited!

Seminar 2: Classroom Atmosphere

Date
_____

Time
_____

Location
_____

A hundred years from now, it will not matter what my bank account balance was, the size of the house I lived in, or the kind of clothes I wore. But the world may be different because I was important in the life of a child.

—Anonymous

Reflections

- How do you see yourself as a teacher?
- Can you name seven characteristics of an inviting classroom?
- What characteristics make a classroom supportive of student achievement?

INTASC Standard 6: Communication and Technology

The teacher uses knowledge of effective verbal, nonverbal, and media communication techniques to foster active inquiry, collaboration, and supportive interaction in the classroom.

Overview

Seminar 2: Classroom Atmosphere

Goal

To provide tips, ideas, suggestions, and activities to enhance the classroom learning environment.

Focus

Today's seminar focuses on strategies for creating a positive classroom environment that supports student achievement and helps build relationships.

Agenda

Welcome Back and Success Stories; Concerns and Questions

Discussion of INTASC Standard 6: Communication and Technology

Seminar 2: Classroom Atmosphere

- Facilitator Strategies
  - □ Body Language 101
  - □ Transitions with Music
  - □ New Teacher in the Movies
  - □ Beginning Bulletin Boards
  - □ Graphic Organizers

Agenda *(Continued)*

- Teacher-Directed Student Activities
  - □ Everyone Has a Story to Tell
  - □ Three-Second Cheers
  - □ Thought of the Day
  - □ Star Student Work

Seminar 2 Reflections

"I'm Ready for Anything" Self-Assessment

INTASC Standard 6: Communication and Technology

The teacher uses knowledge of effective verbal, nonverbal, and media communication techniques to foster active inquiry, collaboration, and supportive interaction in the classroom.

Web-Type Graphic Organizer

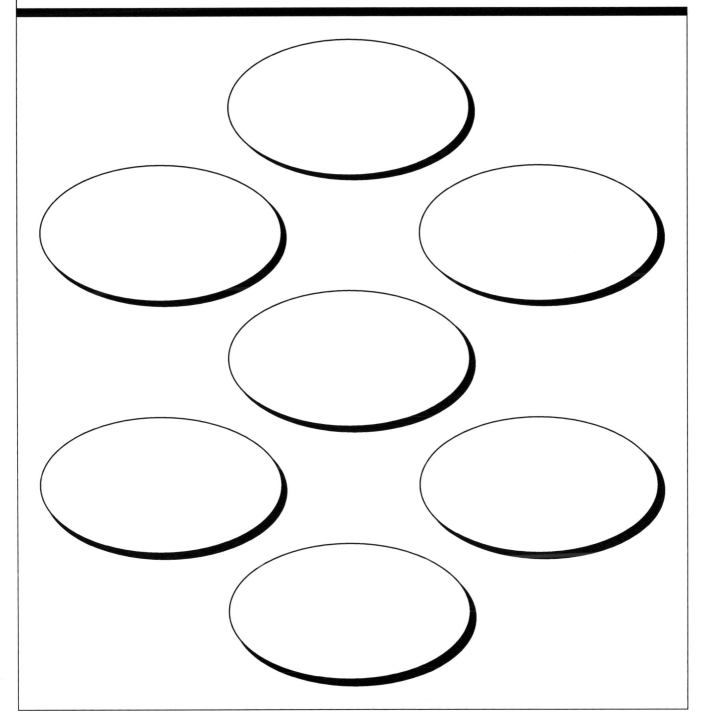

Box Tree
Graphic Organizer

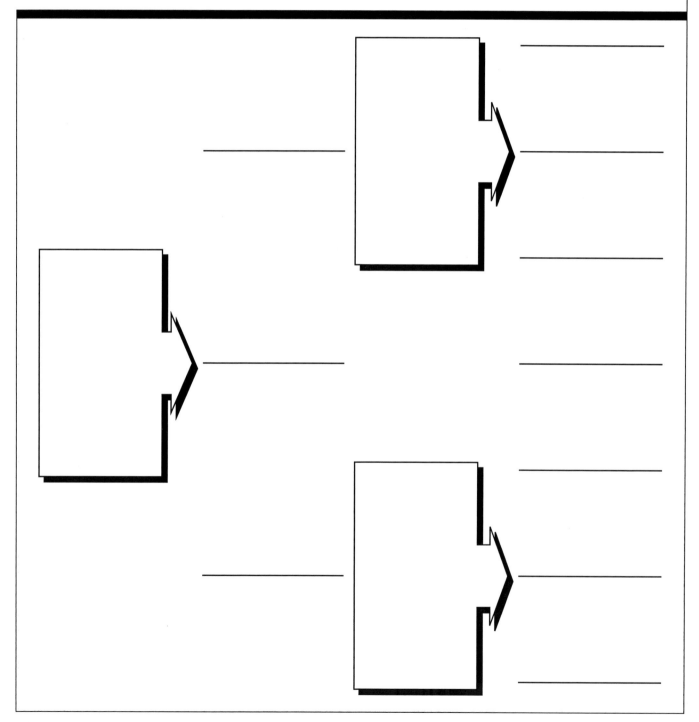

Venn Diagram Graphic Organizer

Cause-and-Effect Graphic Organizer

Cause	Effect

Sequencing
Graphic Organizer

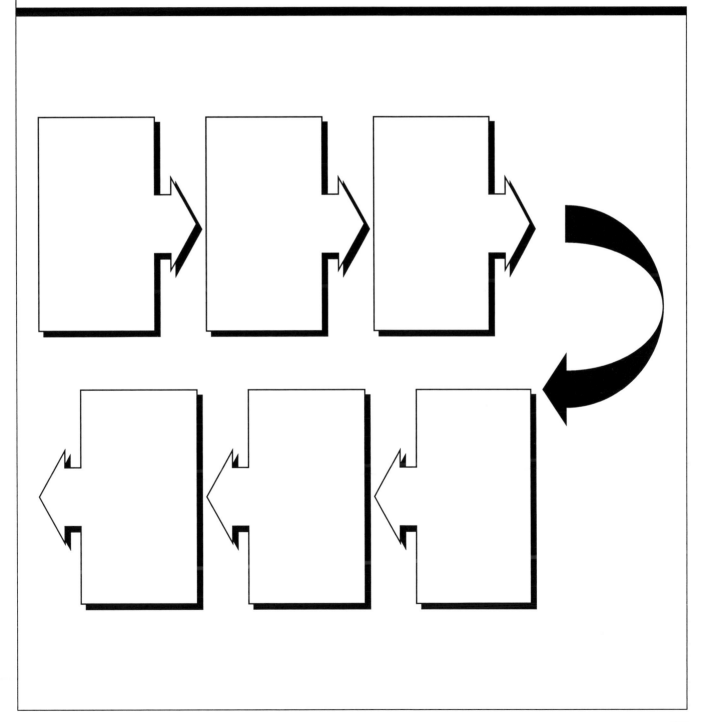

Three-Second Cheers

Silent Cheer Students stand and cheer without making any noise.

Handshake Pairs of students shake hands with a creatively designed handshake.

Golf Clap Individual students clap hands, very quietly.

Pat on the Back Students stand and pat themselves on the back.

Give Myself a Hug Students stand and give themselves a hug.

Hoop Shot Individual students mime taking and making a huge basketball shot.

Take a Bow Students stand and bow several times.

Jump! Students jump in place and cheer.

Walkabout Students walk around the room congratulating others.

March in Place Students march in place to a beat.

Round of Applause Students clap for themselves (giving themselves a round of applause).

You Rock! Students stand, rock back and forth on their feet and say, "You rock!" five times.

Awesome Students jump and yell "Awesome!"

High Five Students stand and give another student a high five.

Sample Quotes for the Classroom

What is success? I think it is a mixture of having a flair for the thing you are doing [and k]nowing that is not enough, that you have got to have hard work and a certain sense of purpose. —Margaret Thatcher

The future belongs to those who prepare for it today. —Malcolm X

I Can is more important than IQ. —Anonymous

We tend to get what we expect. —Norman Vincent Peale

Change is inevitable, except from a vending machine. —Anonymous

Turtles only make progress when they stick out their necks. —Anonymous

Plan your work for today and every day, then work your plan. —Norman Vincent Peale

If at first you don't succeed, try reading the directions. —Anonymous

Don't let what you cannot do interfere with what you can do. —John Wooden

When you get to the end of your rope, tie a knot and hang on. —Franklin D. Roosevelt

A journey of a thousand miles begins with a single step. —Chinese saying

It doesn't matter how slow you go, as long as you don't stop. —Confucius

Learning is not a spectator sport. —Anonymous

It's frustrating when you have all the answers, but nobody bothers to ask you the questions. —Anonymous

Seminar 2 Reflections

Activity: Classroom Crawl

It is important to create an inviting and supportive learning environment for students. You will be going on a classroom adventure to investigate different environments in your school.

Please take the time to rate each room and offer suggestions or comments, keeping INTASC Standard 6 in mind. Use the Classroom Crawl worksheet (*figure 2.11*) and leave the form on the desk for the classroom teacher's review.

INTASC Standard 6: Communication and Technology

The teacher uses knowledge of effective verbal, nonverbal, and media communication techniques to foster active inquiry, collaboration, and supportive interaction in the classroom.

Classroom Crawl

Rating Method: 4 = Impressive   3 = Not bad   2 = Needs improvement   1 = Help!

Rating

General Appearance (e.g., clean, attractive, student-oriented, colorful, inviting, smells good) .... _____

COMMENTS

_____

_____

General Arrangement of the Room (e.g., areas conducive for walking, materials accessible, equipment in place, teacher desk strategically placed) .... _____

COMMENTS

_____

_____

Bulletin Board and Student Work (e.g., current, neat, supports content, area for star work) .... _____

COMMENTS

_____

_____

The Focus Board (e.g., objective, date, agenda, homework, essential questions, focus activity) .... _____

COMMENTS

_____

_____

TOTAL _____

Self-Assessment

"I'm Ready for Anything" Self-Assessment (Seminar 2)

How Am I Doing?	Personal Comments
What specific things make my classroom inviting and student centered?	
What additional activities or designs can I implement to continue to create a welcoming environment?	
Am I perceived as a structured, respectful educator in my school? Why or why not?	
How am I using graphic organizers to transfer information?	
When did I invite a colleague to visit my room and offer feedback? What decisions can I make based on the feedback information?	
How do I take advantage of "teachable moments"?	
How do my students perceive me? What actions do I need to continue to improve or focus on improving?	
What strategies am I using to promote a positive learning environment?	
Have I decided to use music? How will this decision affect the learning environment?	
What materials do I need to review the general evaluation policies for my district?	
What feedback will I receive to help me continue to grow professionally?	

Seminar ③ Classroom Management

Contents

THERE ARE SOME CHILDREN that you just can't figure out—but you never quit trying. Adam was a very gifted student who was failing every subject in eighth grade. No one seemed to be able to get it through to him that he was "wasting his life." His discipline record was volumes in length, and his parents and I were on a first-name basis because of our numerous conferences and telephone conversations throughout the year. They had done what all parents do: grounded him, taken away everything but food and water, threatened, cajoled . . . and they were ready to give up. I was really tired of Adam's shenanigans, because I knew his potential.

One day I sat Adam down for a chat. I asked him about his parents taking away the TV; he didn't like TV. I asked about removing the phone; he had no particular friends to call. What about the skateboard? He didn't like hurting himself. Finally I asked him, since all this was gone, what did his parents do next? He replied that they sent him to his room. But without all his stuff, how could that have been fun? He looked directly at me and said, "I like to read, and when I am banished to my room, it is a pleasure to sit and read."

After this revelation, Adam looked at me and begged me not to tell. In one of the many teacher-student negotiations that we all hold near-sacred, I gave Adam three weeks to improve his grades. He graduated ninth grade with all As.

Sometimes we just have to figure out the management that works.

Introduction

Goal To provide positive classroom management strategies and activities that motivate and support student achievement and self-esteem and positively affect student behavior

Time frame Two hours

Agenda

Welcome Back and Success Stories; Concerns and Questions

Discussion of INTASC Standard 5: Motivation and Management

Seminar 3: Classroom Management

Facilitator Strategies

Teacher-Directed Student Activities

Seminar 3 Reflections

"I'm Ready for Anything" Self-Assessment

After Three Survey

CLASSROOM MANAGEMENT IS THE SINGLE most difficult challenge for a beginning teacher, and one of the top reasons why teachers leave the profession. *Classroom management* refers to everything a teacher does to organize time, space, and students so that effective instruction occurs everyday. It was, however, described by one of my new teachers as "herding mosquitoes." Teachers who learn to manage the classroom keep students on task and actively engaged with their work. Beginning teachers often feel that inability to manage their classes is a sign of weakness, so they are often afraid to ask for help. It takes time to develop the skills for managing student behavior, and conversations and demonstrations in this area should be ongoing during the school year.

Being overprepared and overplanned for class will reduce the amount of time spent on behavioral issues. What happens on the first day of school determines the pace of and success during the rest of the year. Posting the rules, rewards, and consequences provides students with a reminder of the teacher's expectations. It is important to establish a working set of procedures from the beginning so that students understand the way the class will operate. Schools and grade-level teams often develop and implement a consistent behavior management plan that is structured for classroom operation. There is no shortage of information on classroom management!

Overview

This seminar concentrates on recognizing positive behavior and providing teachers with simple strategies to implement in their classrooms. Four key guidelines help teachers create an atmosphere of trust and care:

1. Establish the procedures and rules and clearly define acceptable and unacceptable behavior.
2. Consistently implement your expectations.
3. Provide sincere and genuine recognition.
4. Ask for help from the administration. Serious and difficult behavior problems should be addressed with the facilitator and the principal immediately.

HELP YOUR NEW TEACHERS UNDERSTAND

that learning to manage a classroom takes time and practice. Management skills include recognizing what works and building on those principles. Teach seminar participants that their relationship with students is a high predictor of student success. Reassure them that asking for help is expected and viewed as a growth opportunity. Take time to discuss classroom management at every seminar, and spend time visiting participants' classrooms to provide feedback and support.

Preparation

Materials Reproducibles (*figures 3.3–3.6*), craft sticks or index cards, markers, small hand mirrors, *After Three* survey, refreshments, door prizes, Special Request form

THE ACTIVITIES IN THIS SEMINAR BUILD

relationships with students, and the idea of "catch them being good" prevails throughout the strategies. Other focus areas include accountability for management implementation, record-keeping, and documentation. Once all the activities have been modeled, have your new teachers select two to three to implement in the classroom. You will need copies of the following:

- Invitation (*figure 3.1*)
- INTASC Standard 5: Motivation and Management (*see figure A*)
- Seminar 3 Overview (*figure 3.2*)
- Student Behavior Log (*figure 3.3*)
- Seminar 3 Reflections (*figure 3.4*)
- "I'm Ready for Anything" Self-Assessment (*figure 3.5*)
- *After Three* survey (*figure 3.6*)
- Special Request form (*figure D*)

Tip

Punishment is what you find that the kid dislikes.

Tip

Use a video clip to reinforce the topic of classroom management.

Facilitator Strategies

Focus Classroom management.

How to Use Use the following strategies to help new teachers build their classroom management; model the activities and encourage teachers to use them in their classrooms.

Student Behavior Log

Provide a spreadsheet so that conferences, calls, and correspondence can be documented throughout the year. Include all interventions made in the classroom and comments and responses. *See figure 3.3.*

The Ten Commandments of Student Discipline

Discuss the "commandments" of student discipline with your new teachers. Write each of the following statements on index cards (one per card) and pass them out for discussion and the implications of each for classroom atmosphere.

1. I will never yell at my students.
2. I will never nag about behavior.
3. I will consistently enforce the rules.
4. I will let my administrator know when I need help.
5. I will keep a sense of humor.
6. I will find positive behavior in *all* of my students.
7. I will model the behavior I expect from my students.
8. I will seek out additional resources and strategies.
9. I will be organized and well planned every day.
10. I will never, ever give up!

Teacher-Directed Student Activities

Focus Using positive behavior management.

Stand by Me

Close proximity to students lets them know that you are watching and aware of their behavior. Continue with the lesson as you walk toward a student and stand next to his or her seat. Glance down at the student and smile.

Call My Name

Ask a question, survey the classroom, pause, and say a student's name. This allows students time for individual thought and prevents the same student from answering every time.

Positive Telephone Calls and Notes

Create a list of procedures for your classroom. Write each on a card or craft stick. Make another set of cards or sticks with student names. At the end of the teaching block, pull a procedure card and a name card. If the student has met the expectation, call the student's home or send a note with a positive comment. It works well to do this for three or four students per day or block of time.

Positive Directions

Give a direction and look for a student who is following the direction. Say the student's name and restate the direction, then add a "thank you" for the student's behavior.

I Like the Way . . .

Find a student who is following your direction. Say, "I like the way [*student's name*] is [*repeat the direction*]." Follow up with a positive phrase such as "Good job," "Thank you," or "Good work."

Quote

Don't waffle in your decision or you will be dead meat.

—First-year sixth-grade social studies teacher

Tip

Before they misbehave, most students will wait to see how you act and respond to various situations. Make your expectations and procedures very clear and consistent from Day 1.

Walk a Mile in My Shoes

Constantly circulate through the room while students are working and look for opportunities to provide positive acknowledgments. This individual, personalized recognition lets students know that you are aware of their progress.

Eyes in the Back of My Head

Even if you are working with groups of students, you can still recognize good behavior. Scan the room for a student who is following directions. Even if your back is turned to that student, say his or her name and restate the direction. This shows students that you are aware of their progress.

The Look

Practice your "teacher look" by standing in front of a mirror. Learn to make direct eye contact with a student in a way that says: "I know you are doing what you should be doing." This is a nondisruptive strategy for refocusing off-task behavior.

You Are the Star

Incorporate the name of a student who is off task while you are teaching. Use the name in a word problem, statement, or question to redirect his or her attention.

Let's Have a Chat

If positive behavior strategies are failing, talk with the student in an individual, private conference. Take time to listen and determine the underlying reasons for the inappropriate behavior before determining consequences.

Spotlight Colors

Teach students to use red, yellow, and green cups or construction-paper tents to show their needed level of support. Place these on their desks and show how the colors will elicit help from the teacher.

Three Sets of Ears

Students should select three other students to help with the question of the moment. If, after a predetermined amount of time, the group cannot answer the question, the students should signal the teacher for help.

A Picture Is Worth

Create a list of classroom procedures that you expect to be followed in your room. Use a digital camera to take photos of exemplary behavior, and share the behavior through transparencies or a bulletin board with the procedure and class names.

Seminar 3 Reflections

Activity: Four-Square Journal

Use the graphic template (*figure 3.4*) to reflect on individual classroom management. Reflect on the following in relation to an incident that occurred in your classroom:

- Describe what happened.
- Describe what you did and what the student(s) did.
- Describe what you would do differently.
- How can you learn from this experience?

"I'm Ready for Anything" Self-Assessment (Seminar 3)

See figure 3.5.

After Three Survey

Ask participants to complete the *After Three* survey (*figure 3.6*). This provides feedback for review of and possible revisions to the *Ready for Anything* program.

Tip

Tip

Make sure you keep student record cards up to date with correct names, addresses, parent phone numbers, and emergency contacts.

You Are Invited!

Seminar 3: Classroom Management

Keep Up the Good Work!

Many teachers summarize their classroom management strategies in a single word: *respect*.

Date
_____

Time
_____

Location
_____

Reflections

- Be ready to discuss any classroom management issues you have.

- How are you doing with classroom appearance, bulletin boards, wall space, student work, board work, and so on?

- Would you want to be a student in your classroom?

INTASC Standard 5: Motivation and Management

The teacher uses an understanding of individual and group motivation and behavior to create a learning environment that encourages positive social interaction, active engagement in learning, and self-motivation.

Overview

Seminar 3: Classroom Management

Goal

To provide tips, ideas, suggestions, and logistical support for positive classroom management.

Focus

Today's seminar focuses on positive management for effective teaching. It covers classroom management strategies that motivate and support positive student behavior.

Agenda

Welcome Back and Success Stories; Concerns and Questions

Discussion of INTASC Standard 5: Motivation and Management

Seminar 3: Classroom Management

- Facilitator Strategies
  - Student Behavior Log
  - The Ten Commandments of Student Discipline

Agenda (Continued)

- Teacher-Directed Student Activities
  - Stand by Me
  - Call My Name
  - Positive Telephone Calls and Notes
  - Positive Directions
  - I Like the Way . . .
  - Walk a Mile in My Shoes
  - Eyes in the Back of My Head
  - The Look
  - You Are the Star
  - Let's Have a Chat
  - Spotlight Colors
  - Three Sets of Ears
  - A Picture Is Worth

Seminar 3 Reflections

"I'm Ready for Anything" Self-Assessment

After Three Survey

INTASC Standard 5: Motivation and Management

The teacher uses an understanding of individual and group motivation and behavior to create a learning environment that encourages positive social interaction, active engagement in learning, and self-motivation.

Student Behavior Log

Student		Teacher
Period		
Parent		Phone

Date and Time	Problem Behavior	Actions Taken

Seminar 3 Reflections

Activity: Four-Square Journal

Reflect on the following in relation
to an incident that occurred in your classroom.

Describe what happened.	*Describe what you did and what the student(s) did.*
Describe what you would do differently.	*How can you learn from this experience?*

INTASC Standard 5: Motivation and Management

The teacher uses an understanding of individual and group motivation
and behavior to create a learning environment that encourages
positive social interaction, active engagement in
learning, and self-motivation.

Self-Assessment

"I'm Ready for Anything" Self-Assessment (Seminar 3)

How Am I Doing?	Personal Comments
What are the school procedures, rules, consequences, and rewards, and how does my classroom reflect consistency with each?	
What management problems do I have?	
Are my procedures, rules, consequences, and rewards posted in my classroom?	
How does my classroom reflect a positive behavior environment?	
How do my verbal and nonverbal skills reflect my attitude of promoting a positive environment?	
How do I handle the following: ■ *Taking attendance* ■ *Bell activities* ■ *Students entering and exiting the classroom* ■ *Hall passes* ■ *Tardies*	
What strategies have I found to be the most effective with my students?	
What do I need the most support and help with?	

After Three Survey

It is time to reflect back on the past three seminars and what you have accomplished during that time. Spend a few minutes and answer the following questions in the graphic organizer. Your input will help the development of the program and assist the organizers to supply what is needed for your professional growth.

What have I learned from the past three seminars?	*How can I effectively use the strategies and activities?*
In what areas do I perceive myself making progress?	*What are three goals for the next few months?*
What do I like most about the seminars and the Ready for Anything *process?*	*What two suggestions can I give to improve the process?*

Seminar Strategic Planning and Lesson Design

Contents

I HAD THE PRIVILEGE OF WORKING WITH an elementary school on teaming and establishing positive learning communities within the school. The next year, the same school requested a better method of organizing and teaching the overwhelming number of state standards and objectives in the curriculum. I asked this staff to bring all the curriculum guides, pacing calendars, state and local standards, and assessment tools that they had used in the past year: We were going to distill this huge amount of information and, ultimately, create a plan for effective and efficient instruction.

At the beginning of our sessions, all grade levels were seated in the media center with the exception of fourth grade, which was conspicuously late. A few moments, the door opened and in marched the fourth-grade folks, who announced that they had had to take a little time to collect all the requested materials. In with them came a beautiful, bright-red wheelbarrow brimming over with binders, printouts, documents, and more such stuff. It made the point instantly!

Introduction

Goal To provide tips, ideas, suggestions, and logistical support for planning and lesson design

Time frame Two hours

Agenda

Welcome Back and Success Stories; Concerns and Questions

Discussion of INTASC Standard 7: Planning

Seminar 4: Strategic Planning and Lesson Design

Facilitator Strategy: Planning for Short- and Long-Range Goals

Facilitator Strategy: Effective Lesson Design and Essential Components

Seminar 4 Reflections

"I'm Ready for Anything" Self-Assessment

YOU CAN EITHER FAIL TO PLAN OR PLAN TO fail in educational arenas. Effective teaching begins with effective planning and is accomplished through a systematic process. There is certainly no shortage of curriculum guides, state documents, assessments, or instructional strategies, all of which are available to teachers. All 50 states have established academic content standards specifying what a student is expected to know and be able to do in grades K–12. Although the terminology may vary in each document, the accountability imposed on schools by the No Child Left Behind Act requires that all students demonstrate proficiency in reading and math by the end of the 2013–2014 school year. For beginning teachers, though, deciding what to teach, when to teach it, and how to teach it can be a daunting task, especially when they are trying to learn so many other skills and strategies at the same time.

Simple strategic planning allows teachers to identify the standards and objectives that must be taught, and to organize each within an identified timeline of strategies and assessments. Once the standards and objectives are mapped out in a year-long calendar, strategies for effectively teaching the standards can be incorporated into daily lesson plans. Lesson plans serve as a teacher's blueprint for communicating standards and objectives to the students. Numerous formats for lesson design are available, but all contain components to help make learning meaningful and purposeful. Again, the terminology may vary, but these components usually include: focus or anticipatory set; objective; teacher input; modeling; guided practice, with checking for understanding; independent practice; and summary.

Overview

Most new teachers, especially those who are entering with no teaching experience or coursework, have not been exposed to the content standards (that is, what students should know and be able to do). One of the most difficult tasks in developing qualified educators is providing time for them to internalize the content, recognize the importance of planning, and plan delivery of the material. Although the planning process presented in this seminar may seem mundane and tedious, an extensive content review will prove to be a valuable tool for new teachers as they devise the instructional program for the year.

THE NINE STEPS COVERED IN THIS SEMINAR

represent the beginning of a more complex and detailed review of the standards and objectives, essential questions, big ideas, and performance assessments. We strongly suggest that, after new teachers have a solid grasp of curriculum planning, they move forward with an advanced analysis of the standards and objectives. Douglas B. Reeves, author of *101 Questions & Answers about Standards, Assessment, and Accountability* (2004, p. 7), states that:

> *The most important reason for you to support academic stan-dards in your school is that the standards are a fair and effective way to give students the "rules of the game" when they are in school. Students know what is expected of them, and the definition of success is never a mystery. In the classes taught by these outstanding teachers, student achievement soars because everyone knows that success is defined by the achievement of a standard, and not merely by beating other students or guessing what the teacher wants.*

Larry Ainsworth, author of *Power Standards* (2004) and *"Unwrap-ping" the Standards* (2003), clearly articulates a systematic and balanced approach to distinguishing which standards are essential for student success. His process for "unwrapping" the standards identifies, for educators, the key concepts and skills necessary for instruction and learning. Once new teachers have a basic under-standing of the state standards and objectives, they will find the process described in these references to be absolutely invaluable in understanding what students need to know and be able to do.

In the vertical articulation of the nine steps, a teacher is also asked to identify specific classroom strategies and assessments that will effectively provide data on what has and has not been mastered by students. The seminar also sets aside time for lesson design discussions that emphasize the essential components of effective instructional plans. For those districts that have pacing and alignment guides, these nine steps provide basic knowledge about the effective planning and organizing of content information. If your district does not have pacing or alignment guides, work with grade and content levels to develop an instructional plan so that the standards and objectives are mapped out and taught during the year, with time built in for ongoing assessments. Create a schedule for reviewing the actual implementation, through detailed lesson plans, of standards and objectives in daily

Tip

Good lesson plans all include: objective, warm-up, link to prior knowledge, teacher input and activities, guided and indepen-dent practice, and assessment.

instructional presentations. Place the strategic planning calendars in a location for other teachers to observe and integrate content topics.

Preparation

Materials State/district/local goals, learning standards, curriculum guides, pacing charts, assessment materials, school and district calendar, testing calendar, sticky notes, poster-size calendar (per grade level), samples of exemplary lesson plans and/or design, reproducibles (*figures 4.3–4.8*), refreshments, door prizes, Special Request form

TODAY'S SEMINAR FOCUSES on short- and long-range planning and organization of the standards and objectives. Effective lesson design components are included in the seminar, which presents a very simple process for organizing and arranging the standards and objectives taught during the year. You will need copies of the following:

- Invitation (*figure 4.1*)
- INTASC Standard 7: Planning (*see figure A*)
- Seminar 4 Overview (*figure 4.2*)
- Reproducibles (*figures 4.3–4.6*)
- Seminar 4 Reflections (*figure 4.7*)
- "I'm Ready for Anything" Self-Assessment (*figure 4.8*)
- Special Request form (*figure D*)

Tip

Help your new teachers understand the rationale underlying the state and district standards and objectives in their curriculum and planning guides. Provide a copy of the state and district goals and standards and take the time to review and discuss their importance.

Facilitator Strategy: Planning for Short- and Long-Range Goals

Focus Strategic planning.

How to Use Use the following strategy to help teachers improve and practice their planning skills.

Nine Easy Steps to Standards and Objectives

Work through the nine steps of the strategic planning model (*figure 4.3*) using your state and local standards and objectives. This simple process allows teachers to visually see the "big picture" of annual curriculum planning. Take time to write out the goals and objectives and include them on the strategic planning template (*figure 4.4*). Add the strategies and assessments in the same way to create a graphic organizer for planning and teaching.

Facilitator Strategy: Effective Lesson Design and Essential Components

Focus Creating and delivering effective lessons.

How to Use Use the following strategy to help teachers improve and practice their lesson design skills.

Effective Lesson Design

Discuss the components of an effective lesson and provide examples of each component. Use the lesson design template (*figure 4.5*) as a sample, or use one from your school or district. A sample lesson plan may help teachers see how theory gets put into practice. *See figure 4.6.*

Seminar 4 Reflections

Activity: It's All About Time

Using the face and times of a clock, label 12 planning and instructional priorities or nonnegotiables for effective teaching. Discuss each with the group. *See figure 4.7.*

"I'm Ready for Anything" Self-Assessment (Seminar 4)

See figure 4.8.

Tip

Take your beginning teachers on a field trip to another school to visit exemplary classrooms.

You Are Invited!

Seminar 4: Strategic Planning and Lesson Design

Date
_____

Time
_____

Location
_____

Life is 10 percent what happens to you and 90 percent how you respond to it.

—Lou Holtz

Reflections

- Reflect back on your best lesson.

- Time + patience + planning = student success.

- How is building relationships important to student success?

INTASC Standard 7: Planning

The teacher plans instruction based upon knowledge of subject matter, students, the community, and curriculum goals.

Overview

Seminar 4: Strategic Planning and Lesson Design

Goal

To provide tips, ideas, suggestions, and logistical support for planning and effective lesson design.

Focus

Today's seminar focuses on short- and long-range planning and organization of the standards and objectives. Effective lesson design components are covered as well.

Agenda

Welcome Back and Success Stories; Concerns and Questions

Discussion of INTASC Standard 7: Planning

Seminar 4: Strategic Planning and Lesson Design

- Facilitator Strategy: Planning for Short- and Long-Range Goals
  - □ Nine Easy Steps to Standards and Objectives

Agenda *(Continued)*

- Facilitator Strategy: Effective Lesson Design and Essential Components
  - □ Effective Lesson Design

Seminar 4 Reflections

"I'm Ready for Anything" Self-Assessment

INTASC Standard 7: Planning

The teacher plans instruction based upon knowledge of subject matter, students, the community, and curriculum goals.

Strategic Planning Steps

Strategic Planning Step	Essential Question	Implementation	Going Beyond with Great Resources
1	Why should we be involved with strategic instructional planning?	Discuss the rationale for strategic planning and organization of the content standards and objectives.	Provide copies of curriculum content standards used by your state and district.
2	What are the standards and objectives that should be taught to during the year?	Review all the content standards and objectives so that teachers understand what the student should know and be able to do by the end of the year.	*Power Standards* by Larry Ainsworth (2004).
3	Based on data, on which objectives and standards are our students the strongest and the weakest?	Identify the specific content objectives that students have mastered or for which they need additional support.	*Accountability in Action: A Blueprint for Learning Organizations, 2d ed.,* by Douglas B. Reeves (2004).
4	How do we organize the standards and objectives so that we teach students what they need to be successful?	Use the strategic planning template (*figure 4.4*) to map out the content. Use sticky notes, if desired, to visually illustrate the number and complexity of the standards.	*Power Standards* by Larry Ainsworth (2004).
5	How long do we teach each standard and objective?	Discuss the nature of the standard and determine a reasonable time frame for each objective (understanding that some objectives overlap and are taught multiple times).	*"Unwrapping" the Standards* by Larry Ainsworth (2003).
6	How do we map out the timeline?	Once you have decided how much time should be spent on each objective, use a year-long calendar to create a teaching plan. HINT: Create quarterly, monthly, weekly, and daily plans for teaching the objectives.	

(continues)

Strategic Planning Steps

(Continued)

Strategic Planning Step	Essential Question	Implementation	Going Beyond with Great Resources
7	If we know what to teach, where do we place the instructional strategies?	Review each objective and determine the best instructional practice for student retention and success. Place these practices on the template as appropriate.	*Classroom Instruction That Works* by Robert J. Marzano, Debra J. Pickering, and Jane E. Pollock (2001).
8	How do we get all of this on the lesson plan?	First, map the standards and objectives and determine a time frame; then adjust daily plans to reflect the individual lessons related to the content.	
9	How and when do we assess learning?	Determine the type of assessments (formative and summative) to use with the learning objective. Place these on the template as it relates to the objective. Build the assessments into the instructional calendar and include days for reteaching and additional review of content materials.	■ *101 Questions & Answers about Standards, Assessment, and Accountability* by Douglas B. Reeves (2004). ■ *101 More Questions & Answers about Standards, Assessment, and Accountability* by Douglas B. Reeves (2004). ■ *Holistic Accountability* by Douglas B. Reeves (2001).

Strategic Planning Template

INSTRUCTIONAL STANDARDS

INSTRUCTIONAL OBJECTIVES

INSTRUCTIONAL STRATEGIES

INSTRUCTIONAL ASSESSMENTS

Lesson Plan Template

Teacher _____

Block _____

Date _____

Time	Lesson Component	Activities/Setting		Materials Needed
	State Objective Essential Questions			
	Focus/Review/Warm-Up			
	Focus Lesson/Word of the Day			
	Link to Prior Knowledge			
	Teacher Input/Modeling	What the teacher does	What the student does	

Lesson Plan Template

(Continued)

Time	Lesson Component	Activities/Setting	Materials Needed
	Guided Practice		
	Independent Practice		
	Check for Understanding/ Assessment Homework		
	Modifications for Special Students		
	Summary/Closure		

Reflections and Next Steps

Teacher _____

Subject _____

Date _____

Sample Lesson Plan for Effective Instruction

Time	Component	Activities	Materials
5–10 minutes	Focus/Review/Bell Activity		
2–5 minutes	Essential Questions		
1–2 minutes	Objective		
5–10 minutes	Focus Lesson		
15–20 minutes	Teacher Input		
15–20 minutes	Guided Practice		
15–20 minutes	Independent Practice		
5–10 minutes	Check for Understanding/Assessment		
1–3 minutes	Summary, Homework		

Seminar 4 Reflections

Activity: It's All About Time

Using the face and times of a clock, label 12 planning and instructional priorities or nonnegotiables for effective teaching. Discuss each with the group.

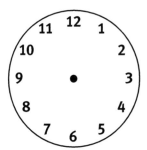

INTASC Standard 7: Planning

The teacher plans instruction based upon knowledge of subject matter, students, the community, and curriculum goals.

Self-Assessment

"I'm Ready for Anything" Self-Assessment (Seminar 4)

How Am I Doing?	Personal Comments
How do I plan to include the standards and goals in my yearly instructional plan?	
Are the goals and objectives clearly related to my short- and long-range plans?	
What are the major obstacles in planning a timely lesson?	
What kind of analyses have I incorporated into the evaluation of lesson effectiveness?	
What methods of instructional presentation do I use most often?	
What additional methods of instructional presentation should I explore?	
What component of lesson design is the most challenging to me?	
What component of lesson design do I consistently do well?	
Who has helped me critique my short- and long-range plans?	
How can I modify my plans and lessons to meet the needs of my students?	
What additional resources can I find to improve the quality of my instructional presentation?	

Seminar The Engaging Classroom

Contents

EVERY OTHER WEDNESDAY WAS "WESLEY DAY." He was a quiet, respectful African-American student in my highly gifted earth science class. Wesley had lots of friends and was always involved in group work and projects for the class, but never spoke out or volunteered to talk aloud. I realized that I wasn't challenging Wesley in class, but I knew that he loved to build models and work on things, so one day I suggested that he bring in something that he had made. When he did, we were all amazed at what we saw! I'm not sure what it was, but it made noise, blew smoke, moved, and flashed lights. The questions from his classmates poured in, and Wesley proudly took time to answer each—and we still wanted more. After several weeks, one of the other students asked Wesley how he got to be so smart; Wesley said, "I read," and nothing more.

We learned more from the quiet nature of a self-motivated child than from all the content in the 679 pages of the earth science textbook. Wesley became a high school chemistry teacher and I am thankful for the opportunity to have made a difference with this student.

Introduction

Goal To provide tips, ideas, suggestions, and logistical support for engaging students in learning.

Time frame Two hours

Agenda

Welcome Back and Success Stories; Concerns and Questions

Discussion of INTASC Standard 4: Multiple Instructional Strategies

Seminar 5: The Engaging Classroom

Teacher-Directed Student Activities: Linguistic Activities

Teacher-Directed Student Activities: Kinesthetic Activities

Teacher-Directed Student Activities: Visual Activities

Seminar 5 Reflections

"I'm Ready for Anything" Self-Assessment

ALL TEACHERS WANT THEIR STUDENTS

to learn and be successful. New teachers often enter the profession with little or no experience in designing instructional strategies that engage, motivate, or challenge the student. They may have been exposed to an expert's demonstration of a strategy, but find it difficult to replicate that strategy in the classroom. Teachers need to understand that a working knowledge of the curriculum precedes the implementation of any strategies or activities, and that effective instruction encompasses a wide range of engagement practices.

Overview

Today's seminar focuses on easy-to-implement, time-friendly strategies that engage and actively involve students in learning. During the seminar, the facilitator models the strategies and schedules time so that each teacher has an opportunity to practice some of the strategies during the remainder of the year.

Preparation

Materials Music and music player, sticky notes, reproducibles (*figures 5.3 – 5.9*), nonfiction text selection, refreshments, door prizes, Special Request form

ALTHOUGH THERE ARE HUNDREDS OF strategies for the classroom, the following simple, easy-to-implement strategies target linguistic, kinesthetic, and visual learning styles, and can be used across all content areas. Allow your teachers to select three or four of the strategies from this seminar to use in their classrooms; have them share their impressions of effectiveness with the group at the next seminar. You will need copies of the following:

- Invitation (*figure 5.1*)
- INTASC Standard 4: Multiple Instructional Strategies (*see figure A*)
- Seminar 5 Overview (*figure 5.2*)
- Reproducibles for teacher-directed student activities (*figures 5.3–5.7*)
- Seminar 5 Reflections (*figure 5.8*)
- "I'm Ready for Anything" Self-Assessment (*figure 5.9*)
- Special Request form (*figure D*)

Tip

Help new teachers understand that the traditional monotone lecture style of teaching may not motivate or engage today's learners. Share the different learning styles, and emphasize that instructional presentation should include a variety of strategies to meet individual learners' needs.

Tip

Use multiple teaching methods to reach all students. Some lecture is fine, but make sure that each student has the opportunity to explore your content through her or his specific learning modality.

Teacher-Directed Student Activities: Linguistic Activities

Focus Linguistic learning modalities.

Tell Me What You Know

Present the class with a topic for discussion. Ask students to brainstorm all that they know about the topic and list whatever they come up with on the board. Ask questions such as: "How do you know?" and "What makes you think so?" After creating a list of terms, facts, and statements, have students read an appropriate nonfiction text selection to further their knowledge. *See figure 5.3.*

Word Splatter

Select vocabulary words, numbers, or phrases from a nonfiction text and randomly write them on the board or an overhead transparency. Ask students to organize or categorize the terms as they relate to the content topic. Accept all answers and discuss how each could relate to the text. Read the full text selection from which the words were drawn for fuller understanding. *See figure 5.4.*

Writing with a Heart

Present a topic to the students. At your signal, students write about that topic on a piece of paper, for a given time limit, with a continuous motion—that is, without lifting the pen or pencil from the paper. At no point does the tip of the writing utensil leave the paper.

This is an endurance strategy for test-taking that helps students learn persistence for the end-of-grade writing test. Start with a small increment of time (15 seconds) and gradually increase it up to 2 minutes of continuous writing.

Answer First

"Answer First" is a unique approach to student thinking, presented in the *Jeopardy* style of questioning. Give students an answer to a content-related topic, and have them generate multiple questions that correspond to the answer. Interdisciplinary connections are encouraged as students expand beyond the traditional content.

3–2–1 Go!

At the end of a lesson, ask students to respond to the following three statements:

1. List the three most important things you learned.
2. Write two questions you still have about the content.
3. Tell one strategy that will help you remember this material.

Vocabulary Web

Place a graphic organizer (*figure 5.3*) on the overhead or board. The center circle contains the word or topic to be discussed. Around the center, students write a definition, illustrate the word or topic, use the word or topic in a sentence, and give a real-world example.

Tip

It is okay to stop the creativity and social engagement if the class is not following rules and procedures. This might be a good time for the textbook and paper and pencil.

Tip

Always have a warm-up or "bell" activity for students to do when entering the classroom. This is a great behavioral strategy and focusing tool.

Teacher-Directed Student Activities: Kinesthetic Activities

Focus Kinesthetic learning modalities.

Shake-Rattle-Roll

Play a music selection while students circulate throughout the classroom. When the music stops, pose a question and allow students to share their answers. Continue for up to 10 questions.

Simon Says

This strategy is played like the traditional children's game. Create a series of true/false statements and read them to the class. If the statement is true, students stand up. If the statement is false, students sit down. Rationales for their answers are discussed. Play continues for a specified amount of review time.

Eyeballs Up/Eyeballs Down

Develop a set of true/false statements relating to your content area. If the statement is true, students roll their eyes up toward the ceiling. If the statement is false, students roll their eyes down toward the floor. Those who do not know the answer should look directly at the teacher.

ABCD Assessment

This activity can be done individually or with pairs of students. Each student (or student pair) is given a card marked with the letters A, B, C, and D (*figure 5.6*). During a review lesson, pose a series of multiple-choice questions. Students should think about their answers and then, when called upon as a group, hold up the letter representing their choice. Make your assessment by doing a quick visual check of the classroom.

Aerobic Spelling

Use words related to the content or from a word wall for review. State the word and have students repeat it three times (as a group). Then spell the word for the students, saying each letter aloud. If the letter is a consonant, students stand up. If the letter is a vowel, students sit down. Proceed through the spelling fairly quickly.

Prediction Sides

Present a series of agree/disagree statements for discussion before the class reads a text portion or article. Label three areas of the room with "agree," "disagree," or "uncertain." After they read each statement, give students time to decide if they agree with, disagree with, or are uncertain about it. Students then move to the area of the room representing their answer. Hold students accountable for their decisions. After completing the statement exercise, reread the text for fuller understanding.

Teacher-Directed Student Activities: Visual Activities

Focus Visual learning modalities.

Video Tic-Tac-Toe

Before viewing a video presentation, give students a tic-tac-toe grid with questions or statements in each grid cell related to the content of the video. Use the grid contents to guide students in discussions before, during, and after viewing the video presentation. You may award points for three-in-a-row completion. *See figure 5.7.*

Do the Doodle

After determining the desired content topic, put a doodle-type line or drawing on the board or overhead. Have students copy the doodle and then demonstrate their knowledge of the content by incorporating that knowledge into a drawing based on the doodle.

Seminar 5 Reflections

Activity: What Would [*Name*] Do to Learn This?

Place the names of famous people on slips of paper and allow students to select one each. Talk about special needs and learning differences with students. Identify specific students in your class who need additional methods for learning. *See figure 5.8.*

"I'm Ready for Anything" Self-Assessment (Seminar 5)

See figure 5.9.

Tip

Use every moment to teach. If you waste 5 minutes a day in a 180-day school year, you will have wasted 900 minutes, or the equivalent of 150 teachable hours.

You Are Invited!

Seminar 5: The Engaging Classroom

Time to Celebrate!

Goodies ▪ *Fun* ▪ *Food*

Date
_____

Time
_____

Location
_____

Reflections

- Would you want to be a student in your classroom?
- How do you learn best?

INTASC Standard 4: Multiple Instructional Strategies

The teacher understands and uses a variety of instructional strategies to encourage student development of critical thinking, problem solving, and performance skills.

Overview

Seminar 5: The Engaging Classroom

Goal

To provide tips, ideas, suggestions, and logistical support for engaging students in learning.

Focus

Today's seminar focuses on easy-to-implement, time-friendly strategies that engage and actively involve students in learning.

Agenda

Welcome Back and Success Stories; Concerns and Questions

Discussion of INTASC Standard 4: Multiple Instructional Strategies

Seminar 5: The Engaging Classroom

- Teacher-Directed Students Activities: Linguistic Activities
    □ Tell Me What You Know
    □ Word Splatter
    □ Writing with a Heart
    □ Answer First
    □ 3–2–1 Go!
    □ Vocabulary Web

Agenda (Continued)

- Teacher-Directed Student Activities: Kinesthetic Activities
    □ Shake-Rattle-Roll
    □ Simon Says
    □ Eyeballs Up/Eyeballs Down
    □ ABCD Assessment
    □ Aerobic Spelling
    □ Prediction Sides
- Teacher-Directed Student Activities: Visual Activities
    □ Video Tic-Tac-Toe
    □ Do the Doodle

Seminar 5 Reflections

"I'm Ready for Anything" Self-Assessment

INTASC Standard 4: Multiple Instructional Strategies

The teacher understands and uses a variety of instructional strategies to encourage student development of critical thinking, problem solving, and performance skills.

Name

Date

What Do You Know About? Graphic Organizer

What Do You Know About?

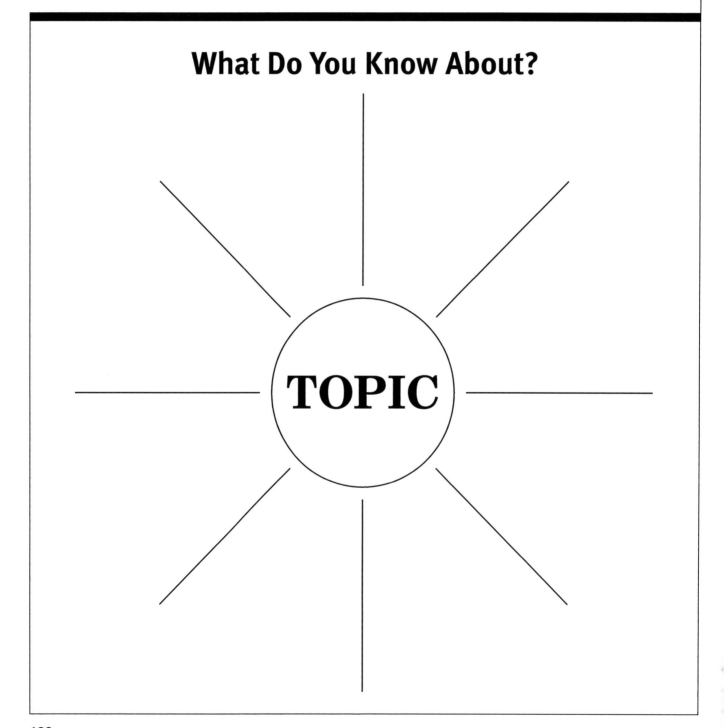

TOPIC

Word Splatter Graphic Organizer

Word Splatter

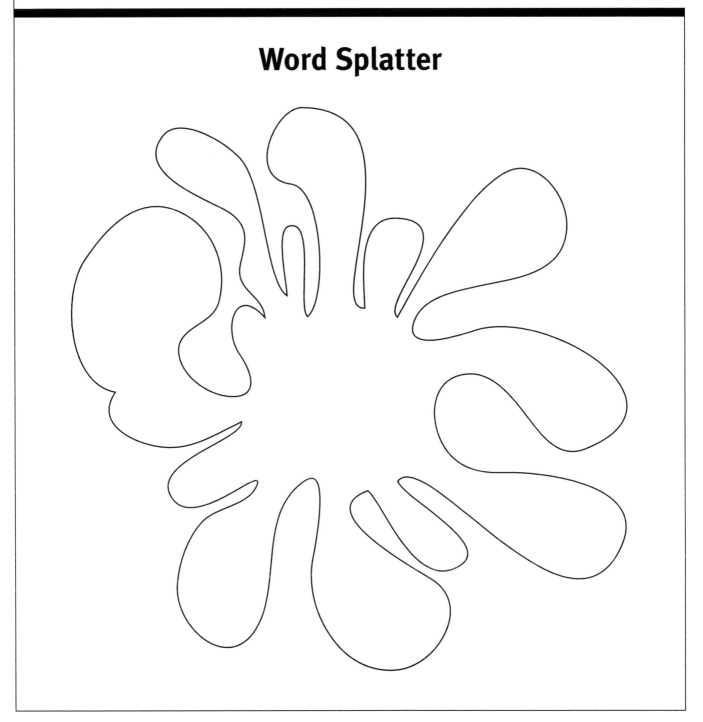

Name _____

Date _____

Vocabulary Web

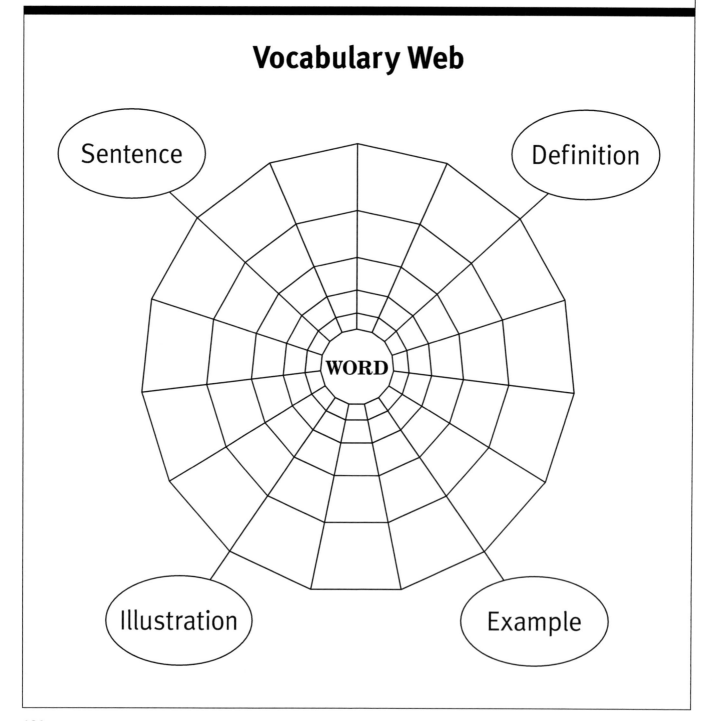

Vocabulary Web

Sentence

Definition

WORD

Illustration

Example

ABCD Assessment Cards

A

B

ABCD Assessment Cards

C

D

Video Tic-Tac-Toe

fact	One thing my friend knows	fact
ONE QUESTION	TOPIC	*One Interesting Observation*
fact	*One thing I already know*	fact

Seminar 5 Reflections

Activity: What Would [*Name*] Do to Learn This?

If the people listed below were in your classroom, how would you address their learning needs? Do the students in your class have similar talents and abilities? Talk about how the strategies can engage the different learning styles.

Michelangelo   Beethoven
Abraham Lincoln   Mother Teresa
Shakespeare   Charles Darwin
Thomas Edison   Elvis Presley
Martin Luther King, Jr.

INTASC Standard 4: Multiple Instructional Strategies
The teacher understands and uses a variety of instructional strategies to encourage student development of critical thinking, problem solving, and performance skills.

Self-Assessment

"I'm Ready for Anything" Self-Assessment (Seminar 5)

How Am I Doing?	Personal Comments
Have I reflected on the need for a variety of strategies in my lessons?	
What have I read about learning styles and modalities of learning?	
How did I survey my students to discover their learning preferences?	
What was my learning style as a student?	
What strategies have I planned to use in my lesson?	
What materials do I need to implement the strategy?	
How have I explained the strategy to the students?	
Have I planned to use or practice the strategy at least three times?	
How did the students react to the strategy?	
How do I know that learning occurred?	
Have I shared the strategy with my colleagues?	
What resources did I use to find additional strategies?	

Seliminar Observations and Evaluations

Contents

I WAS KNOWN AS ADMIRAL HOWARD of the *USS Alexander.* My oceanography class was run like the U.S. Navy, with promotions, in-class seafaring excursions, and a nautical décor. I was proud of my admiral's cap, wore it every day with dignity, and my students loved being in the "navy."

During one of these years, I had the opportunity to participate in the Career Development Incentive Program, which meant that "observers" would enter the room; stay for the entire teaching block; record every word, breath, and movement that I and the students made; not speak or make eye contact; leave; and send a sealed rating scale back through the mail. This evaluation was tied to a monetary bonus incentive—but only if you achieved exemplary ratings.

I happened to be teaching seventh-grade oceanography when "The Man" came to observe. "The Man," who had a reputation of being cold and very harsh in his ratings, sat in the back of the room, wrote pages and pages, and never looked at me. I was so unnerved that I forgot the last of the sacred steps in the mandated lesson plan. One of my students, who knew that "The Man" was in the back, looked up at me with five minutes left in the period and quietly said, "Summary." The students knew that if I didn't follow the steps of the lesson design and say the key words, I would be marked down and receive a poor rating. I didn't hear him the first time, so he coughed and said it again. I looked at this student, and then announced to the class that we would now summarize the lesson. When "The Man" left, there was a huge sigh of relief and laughter from all.

All the teachers in the program wanted to achieve exemplary ratings; after all, we thought we were the best of the best. When the scoring letter came one week later, it was addressed to "Admiral Lynn Howard—USS Alexander"! I learned that "The Man" was a real teacher with a great sense of humor, and that I should never judge someone until I knew the facts.

Introduction

Goal To provide tips, ideas, suggestions, and logistical support for better understanding of the components of required teacher evaluations

Time frame Two hours

Agenda

Welcome Back and Success Stories; Concerns and Questions

Discussion of INTASC Standards 1–10

Seminar 6: Observations and Evaluations

Facilitator Strategy: Teacher Performance

Facilitator Strategies: Evidence of Effective Teaching

Seminar 6 Reflections

"I'm Ready for Anything" Self-Assessment

After Three Survey

BEGINNING TEACHERS STATE THAT observations and evaluations are the number-one cause of educational stress. Induction programs typically do not communicate what teacher appraisal instruments expect and measure, and evaluations are conducted and filed without teachers being provided the skills and knowledge needed to effectively do the job that is being evaluated.

A useful evaluation process should provide teachers with feedback on their instructional presentations, use of time, class management, and organizational skills. The purpose of evaluations should be twofold: to measure teacher competence and ability, and to facilitate appropriate professional development and growth. A meaningful and purposeful evaluation should strike a balance between criticism and approval.

The opportunity to learn strategies and make changes in the classroom should be the primary focus of observations. In addition, a chance to observe master teachers affords new teachers models of excellence as they develop their teaching and relationship styles with students.

Overview

This seminar provides an opportunity for the facilitator to review the state and district evaluation instruments and the INTASC Standards in detail. It also guides participants in taking an in-depth look at evidence of effective teaching, using a series of templates covering management of time, behavior, instruction, monitoring and feedback, and noninstructional responsibilities. The template tools are designed to use essential questions for discussion and growth.

Preparation

Materials Copy of state/district evaluation instruments for teachers, reproducibles (*figures 6.3–6.12*), index cards, *After Three* survey, refreshments, door prizes, Special Request form

TODAY'S SEMINAR FOCUSES on state and local

requirements for teacher observations and evaluations. It is intended to help take the fear and uncertainty out of observations and evaluations, and to give new teachers tools with which to evaluate their own progress. You will need copies of the following:

- Invitation (*figure 6.1*)
- INTASC Standards 1–10 (*figure A*)
- Seminar 6 Overview (*figure 6.2*)
- Reproducibles for facilitator strategies (*figures 6.3–6.9*)
- Seminar 6 Reflections (*figure 6.10*)
- "I'm Ready for Anything" Self-Assessment (*figure 6.11*)
- *After Three* survey (*figure 6.12*)
- Special Request form (*figure D*)

Tip

Help your new teachers understand that observations and evaluations are tools for growth and often required by the state and district. Use the assessment checklist with each seminar to discuss strengths and areas for improvement. Take time to review the "Evidences of Effective Teaching" essential questions and provide additional support as needed on a regular basis. Never, ever belittle new teachers for their endeavors and efforts.

Facilitator Strategy: Teacher Performance

Focus What new teachers need to know about observations and evaluations.

How to Use Use the following strategy to help teachers better understand the components of required teacher evaluations.

Teacher Appraisal Instruments

Provide a copy of the state and/or local evaluation instruments for participants to discuss. Allow them to generate questions about the instruments and discuss those questions.

Facilitator Strategies: Evidence of Effective Teaching

Focus Instructional presentations

How to Use Use the following strategies to help teachers improve their effectiveness and apply best professional practices.

Classroom Checklist

Use the "Classroom Checklist" from the Center for Performance Assessment (*figure 6.3*) as a starting point in your discussion of professional practices in effective classrooms. Take time to discuss each practice and model examples, if applicable. Remember that these practices represent the highest standards for achievement and that new teachers should work toward "exemplary" status in each.

Just the Facts!

Use the "Evidence of Effective Teaching" worksheets (management of time, behavior, instruction, monitoring and feedback, and noninstructional duties) for building skills and knowledge that exemplify effective teaching. Review each component, taking time to model the evidences and answer the essential questions. Use the template worksheets in conferencing discussions and as documentation of professional growth. Have participants select three targeted areas to improve during the next month. Ask each new teacher to be ready to share with the group his or her process for growth. *See figures 6.4–6.8.*

Tip

Leave a positive note each time you visit a classroom.

Classroom Response

Use the classroom response form (*figure 6.9*) for informal observations made during a walk-through or short visits during the instructional period. Provide time for discussion during each new teacher's individual conferencing time. *See also figure 1.9.*

Seminar 6 Reflections

Activity: Don't Step on My T.O.E.S. (Teacher Observation and Evaluation Survival)

Write the suggested question prompts (*figure 6.10*) on cards and pass the cards out to your teachers. Provide time for discussion in groups of three; select the most meaningful prompt to share with the whole group.

"I'm Ready for Anything" Self-Assessment (Seminar 6)

See figure 6.11.

After Three Survey

Provide time for participants to complete the *After Three* survey (*figure 6.12*). Their responses should be used to guide review and revision of the program.

Tip

Help new teachers understand that observations are a chance to really show off what they are doing that is working well for them.

You Are Invited!

Seminar 6: Observations and Evaluations

*Feedback from observations is an opportunity
for professional growth.*

Date
_____

Time
_____

Location
_____

Reflections

- How do you know if you are a good teacher?

- How do you feel your lesson plans are working?

INTASC Standards 1–10

- Standard 1: Content Pedagogy
- Standard 2: Student Development
- Standard 3: Diverse Learners
- Standard 4: Multiple Instructional Strategies
- Standard 5: Motivation and Management
- Standard 6: Communication and Technology

- Standard 7: Planning
- Standard 8: Assessment
- Standard 9: Reflective Practice: Professional Development
- Standard 10: School and Community Involvement

Overview

Seminar 6: Observations and Evaluations

Goal

To provide tips, ideas, suggestions, and logistical support for better understanding of the components of required teacher evaluations.

Focus

Today's seminar focuses on state and local requirements for teacher observations and evaluations.

Agenda

Welcome Back and Success Stories; Concerns and Questions

Discussion of INTASC Standards 1–10

Seminar 6: Observations and Evaluations

■ Facilitator Strategy: Teacher Performance

□ Teacher Appraisal Instruments

Agenda *(Continued)*

■ Facilitator Strategies: Evidence of Effective Teaching

□ Classroom Checklist

□ Just the Facts!

□ Classroom Response

Seminar 6 Reflections

"I'm Ready for Anything" Self-Assessment

After Three Survey

Classroom Checklist from the Center for Performance Assessment

For each element of Proficient Practice, please indicate with a checkmark that the practice is present.

Component	Evidence of Proficient Practices
1. Standards are highly visible in the classroom. The standards are expressed in language that the students understand.	❑ Relevant standards are posted in the classroom in language that students can understand. ❑ Standards are specifically referenced in lesson plans. ❑ Specific knowledge and skills from the standards are identified. ❑ Student learning activities are clearly aligned with the standards. ❑ Learning objectives/daily questions that are clearly aligned with the standards are stated or posted. ❑ Learning activities are clearly aligned with the standards. ❑ Standards and learning objectives can be accurately and clearly explained by the teacher and student.

2. Examples of "exemplary" and "proficient" student work are displayed throughout the classroom.	❑ Student work directly related to the standards currently being learned is displayed and includes:
	  ❑ Standards that are being demonstrated
	  ❑ Rubric that describes performance expectations
	  ❑ "Score" from the rubric (exemplary, proficient, progressing)
	  ❑ Individual performance tasks, complete assessments, and projects
	  ❑ Work by a variety of students

3. Students can spontaneously explain what "proficient" work means for each assignment.	❑ Students:
	  ❑ Explain the criteria by which their work will be assessed
	  ❑ Locate the rubric or criteria for the current assignment
	  ❑ Use the vocabulary in the rubric to describe their work
	  ❑ Refer to the rubric as they complete the assignment
	❑ Evidence exists of:
	  ❑ Self-assessment or self-reflection using criteria in the rubric
	  ❑ Peer assessment using criteria in the rubric
	  ❑ Feedback to the students that resulted in direct action by the students

4. For every assignment, project, or test, the teacher publishes in advance the explicit expectations for "proficient" work.	❑ Rubric is distributed to students before beginning working on tasks, projects, or assessments.
	❑ Published rubric includes:
	  ❑ Criteria for "Proficient" performance
	  ❑ Criteria related to the standards
	  ❑ Language that is:
	    ❑ Specific ❑ Understandable
	    ❑ Measurable ❑ Matched to task/assignment directions

5. Student evaluation is always done according to the standards and rubric criteria and never done based on a "curve."	❑ Evaluation of student work is done according to a rubric or criteria related to the standards. ❑ Only objective criteria are used to evaluate student work. ❑ Criteria for "Proficient" performance is included and based on academic content standards.

6. The teacher can explain to any parent or stakeholder the specific expectations of students.	❑ For the subjects that the teacher is responsible for, the teacher uses a document that contains specific expectations for students about proficiency in:
	  ❑ Content they are expected to know
	  ❑ Skills they are expected to demonstrate

Classroom Checklist
(Continued)

Component	Evidence of Proficient Practices
7. The teacher has the flexibility to vary the length and quantity of curriculum content on a day-to-day basis in order to ensure that students receive more time on the most critical subjects.	❏ Students are constantly being assessed on their progress towards meeting standards. ❏ The teacher has written evidence of individual students' proficiency on standards. ❏ The teacher knows which students are not proficient on the standards and is able to provide additional time and instructional assistance for the student to demonstrate proficiency. ❏ Performance expectations for all students remain constant even if time allocations and curricular emphases are different.

8. Commonly used standards, such as those for written expression, are reinforced in every subject area. In other words, "spelling always counts"—even in math, science, music, and every other discipline.	❏ Common rubrics that assess the use of conventions:
	  ❏ Have been developed for assessing conventions where appropriate
	  ❏ Are used to evaluate published written assignments in all subject areas

9. Standards-based performance assessments are used in the classroom.	❏ Standards-based performance assessments include:
	  ❏ Standards and grade-level benchmarks being assessed
	  ❏ Tasks within the assessment have individual rubrics
	  ❏ Real-world application for the skills is being assessed

10. The teacher exchanges student work (accompanied by a rubric) with a colleague for review and evaluation at least once every two weeks.	❏ Teaching objectives are influenced by results of collegial review and evaluation of student work. ❏ Teachers collaboratively score a sample of the student work using the rubric, review the scores for the student work, and reach 80% consensus in scoring student work.

11. The teacher provides feedback to students (and parents) about the quality of student work compared to the standards—not compared to other students.	❏ Reporting of grades (either on report cards or in grade books) is standards-based. Where standardized grade reporting systems exist, a supplemental report includes student achievement in relation to the standards.
	❏ Feedback is:
	  ❏ Timely ❏ Clearly related to the rubric
	  ❏ Specific ❏ Reinforcement for high expectations for all students
	  ❏ Clearly related to the standards

12. The teacher helps to build a community consensus in the classroom and with other stakeholders for standards and high expectations of all students.	❏ Teacher encourages and maintains high expectations for all students by allowing students to revise their work to demonstrate achievement of the standards. ❏ Teacher communicates that all students can achieve at high levels. ❏ Teacher provides interactive participation through cooperative learning activities to build a community of learners.
13. The teacher uses a variety of assessment techniques, including, but not limited to, extended written responses, in all disciplines.	❏ Classroom assessment techniques include both traditional assessment (multiple choice, fill-ins, matching) and performance assessment (performance tasks, projects, presentations, extended written responses). ❏ Assessment techniques are aligned with the knowledge and skills contained within the standards.

Notes

Evidence of Effective Teaching—Management of Time

Management of Time	Evidence	Essential Questions	Exemplary	Proficient	Progressing
Teacher has materials, supplies, and equipment ready for instruction	■ Objective, date, and homework posted ■ Lesson plans made and used ■ Audiovisual equipment appropriately used ■ Handouts/worksheets available ■ Lab materials and manipulatives available ■ Supplemental texts available	■ What materials does the teacher need on a daily basis? ■ What techniques does the teacher use to prepare for each lesson?			
Teacher gets class started quickly	■ Bell activity posted ■ Attendance check is quick ■ Student time management expectations are in place	■ What procedures are in place for getting students quickly on task? ■ What techniques does the teacher use to save administrative time? ■ How is academic time managed?			
Teacher makes transitions between activities quickly	■ Quick movement of students from one activity to another ■ Use of a timer ■ Links to prior knowledge ■ Smooth flow of lesson design transition?	■ What procedures are used for activity reorganization? ■ Was time lost from one activity to another? ■ Are materials ready for each transition?			
Teacher maintains high time on task for student learning	■ Schedule/agenda posted ■ Clear directions for activities ■ Frequent teacher monitoring	■ How does the teacher effectively pace the lesson? ■ How does the teacher adjust instruction to meet the needs of each student? ■ How are students engaged in work?			
Teacher carries out noninstructional duties and assignments in a timely manner	■ Team/planning minutes ■ Daily sign-in sheet ■ Report checklists	■ What are the teacher's required duties? ■ What evidence does the teacher use to support his or her involvement with school activities?			

Evidence of Effective Teaching—Management of Behavior

Management of Behavior	Evidence	Essential Questions	Exemplary	Proficient	Progressing
Teacher has established rules and procedures for administrative matters	■ Rules, rewards, consequences posted ■ Procedures are in place for taking attendance, taking up homework, returning work, checking in-class work, receiving make-up work, addressing tardies	■ What administrative matters are done on a daily basis? ■ Is there a consistent pattern?			
Teacher has established rules and procedures for verbal behavior	■ Rules, rewards, consequences posted ■ Procedures are in place for asking questions, responding to the teacher, getting attention, working with partners/groups	■ What verbal rules and procedures are implemented on a daily basis? ■ Is there a consistent pattern?			
Teacher has established rules and procedures for movement	■ Rules, rewards, consequences posted ■ Procedures are in place for forming groups, getting supplies, returning materials	■ What movement rules and procedures are implemented on a daily basis? ■ Is there a consistent pattern?			
Teacher frequently monitors behavior (whole-group, small group, individual)	■ Circulating through the classroom ■ Behavior plan in place for students ■ Visual observations made ■ Verbal cues and recognition given	■ What procedures are in place for documenting behavior? ■ What strategies are used to handle inappropriate behavior?			
Teacher effectively handles inappropriate behavior	■ Rules, rewards, consequences posted ■ Behavior logs/documentation ■ Team minutes ■ Exceptional Children (EC) modifications made	■ What procedures are in place for documenting behavior? ■ What strategies are used to handle inappropriate behavior?			

Evidence of Effective Teaching—Management of Instruction

Management of Instruction	Evidence	Essential Questions	Exemplary	Proficient	Progressing
Teacher has short- and long-range plans	■ Lesson plans ■ Pacing/curriculum guides ■ Team/planning minutes ■ Newsletters and parent communications	■ What materials are used to determine the instructional content of each lesson? ■ How effective are the lesson plans? ■ How consistent is the planning with that of other content/grade-level teachers?			
Teacher links instruction to prior learning	■ Objective stated ■ Previous activity review ■ Relevant examples ■ Student responses and questions	■ How does the teacher connect day-to-day learning? ■ What strategies are used to activate prior knowledge? ■ What types of questions are used to encourage connections?			
Teacher makes content matter meaningful, understandable, and grade-level appropriate	■ Strong knowledge of content ■ Relevant and real-world examples ■ Clear directions and assignments ■ Additional resources, visuals, manipulatives, demonstrations used	■ How does the teacher know that students are learning? ■ How does the teacher adjust instruction to meet students' levels of understanding? ■ How are additional resources used?			
Teacher communicates the lesson fluently, precisely, and correctly	■ Clear and understandable pronunciation ■ Proper grammar and spelling ■ Relevant vocabulary ■ Brisk pace	■ Can students understand what is said verbally? ■ Do the teacher's written and spoken words reflect proper grammar and spelling? ■ Is the level of vocabulary appropriate?			
Teacher provides relevant examples and demonstrations that support the lesson objective(s)	■ Visual and manipulative resources ■ Video and audio segments ■ Additional text ■ Guest speakers	■ How does the teacher determine relevant examples for the lesson? ■ How does the teacher differentiate for the various levels of student understanding?			

Management of Instruction
(Continued)

Management of Instruction	Evidence	Essential Questions	Exemplary	Proficient	Progressing
Teacher asks questions at appropriate levels for student success	■ Lesson plans include levels of questions ■ Bulletin boards/displays ■ Wait Time I and II ■ Clear directions given ■ Verbal and written activities used	■ How does the teacher measure student success? ■ How does the teacher develop the questions to be included in the lesson? ■ How does the teacher incorporate the multiple levels of thinking?			
Teacher makes smooth transitions between activities	■ Materials ready ■ Clear directions given ■ Response time to changing activities ■ Number of student questions	■ How does the teacher connect one activity with the next? ■ How does the end of one lesson connect with the beginning of the next?			
Teacher uses a variety of instructional presentation techniques	■ Use of multiple intelligences in activities ■ Students are provided choices ■ EC modifications made ■ Lesson plans ■ Portfolio of strategies ■ Multiple class arrangements ■ Cooperative learning activities ■ Student work products	■ How does the teacher select the strategies to be used in the lesson? ■ How does the teacher assess the effectiveness of each strategy? ■ How are students involved in the lesson?			
Teacher encourages student accountability	■ Student notebook/grade sheets ■ Portfolios ■ Reflection logs ■ Cooperative learning logs ■ Homework/make-up procedures ■ Motivational programs	■ How does the teacher hold students responsible for their learning? ■ What strategies are used to encourage accountability? ■ What is the home/school connection?			
Teacher adapts instruction for diverse learners	■ Use of multiple instructional presentation techniques ■ EC modification ■ Choices of products	■ What type of learners are in the classroom? ■ What strategies does the teacher use to address students' learning needs?			

Evidence of Effective Teaching—Management of Monitoring and Feedback

Management of Monitoring and Feedback	Evidence	Essential Questions	Exemplary	Proficient	Progressing
Teacher provides feedback on correct or incorrect work or responses	■ Verbal and nonverbal cues ■ Dignifying student errors ■ Effective monitoring	■ How does the teacher respond to student responses? ■ How does the teacher dignify incorrect responses? ■ What strategies does the teacher use to reteach material?			
Teacher regularly provides prompt feedback on in-class and out-of-class work	■ Verbal and nonverbal cues ■ Returned paper/product activities ■ Grades ■ Portfolios/journals ■ Motivational programs ■ Rubrics	■ How does the teacher manage feedback (both in and outside of class)? ■ What strategies does the teacher use to hold students accountable for their work? ■ What system of standards is used?			
Teacher uses verbal and nonverbal communication techniques	■ Teacher's physical location ■ Verbal and nonverbal cues ■ Written notes ■ Response journals ■ Parent logs/documentation	■ What techniques are used to ensure student success? ■ How do students respond to the teacher?			
Teacher develops a method for analyzing student performance	■ Data analysis ■ Rubrics ■ Portfolios ■ Team conference notes	■ How does the teacher disaggregate student data? ■ What modifications are made in lesson plans? ■ How are students held accountable for their learning?			

Evidence of Effective Teaching—Management of Noninstructional Duties

Management of Noninstructional Duties	Evidence	Essential Questions	Exemplary	Proficient	Progressing
Teacher follows standards of learning as outlined by state and local education agencies	■ Standards of learning ■ Lesson plans ■ Team/planning minutes ■ Standards and objectives posted ■ Parent communications	■ What strategies does the teacher use to develop short- and long-range goals? ■ How are the standards and objectives incorporated into the lesson?			
Teacher maintains accurate records	■ Gradebook and grade sheets ■ Progress reports ■ Report cards ■ Discipline logs ■ Running records ■ Parent communications	■ What does the teacher use to reflect on analysis of student achievement? ■ What does the teacher do to support school and local accountability measures?			
Teacher uses available resources	■ Lesson plans ■ Manipulative inventories ■ Community programs ■ Media and audiovisual materials	■ How are additional resources incorporated into the lesson? ■ How are community resources used? ■ What additional materials does the teacher need?			
Teacher builds relationships with community, staff, and students	■ Parent communications ■ PTSA logs ■ Attendance at after-school activities ■ Grade-level planning ■ Professional evaluations ■ School- and district-based communities ■ Professional presentations	■ What is the relationship between the teacher and the community, staff, and students? ■ What strategies does the teacher use to build relationships?			
Teacher participates in professional development	■ Individual growth plan ■ Written and shared synopsis of professional development activities ■ Lesson plan reflections	■ What target areas should the individual growth plan focus on? ■ How does the teacher share new knowledge with others? ■ How does the teacher incorporate new learning ideas?			

Classroom Response Form

Classroom Response Form

| Teacher | | Date |

Instructional Evidence	Observed	Not Observed
Lesson plans		
Materials ready		
Objectives		
Essential questions		
Homework		
Student work		
Word wall		
Student engagement		
Inviting atmosphere		
Teacher monitoring		
Assessments used		
Management plan		
Sustaining feedback		
Evidence of data analysis for differentiation		

Observer

Please write additional comments and information for any category marked "Not Observed":

Seminar 6 Reflections

Activity: Don't Step on My T.O.E.S.
(Teacher Observation and Evaluation Survival)

Look at the following prompts
and think about being observed. Take some time
to discuss with your small group how each prompt relates to
evaluations at the teacher level. Select three that are
significant to you and discuss them with the whole group.

PROMPTS

What I did best today was . . .

It is hard for me to organize . . .

My best management strategy is . . .

I watched _____ do _____ really well . . .

If only I knew . . .

How can . . .

I will do _____ better . . .

I need to see . . .

When do I have the time to . . .

I am struggling with . . .

My problem with time is . . .

I can't seem to get . . .

My thinking changed about . . .

What if . . .

Where will I go to . . .

It is very easy to . . .

I love to . . .

Why can't . . .

INTASC Standards 1–10

Self-Assessment

"I'm Ready for Anything" Self-Assessment (Seminar 6)

How Am I Doing?	Personal Comments
Have I talked with my principal or designee about the required teacher observations and evaluations?	
What is expected during an observation?	
Do I share observer classroom visits with my students?	
What are my strongest areas?	
What are my weakest areas? How can I improve there?	
What happens at mid-year and at the end of the year with my evaluation?	
Who is responsible for observing and evaluating me?	
What happens if I don't do well in a category?	
How do I know that evaluations will be and remain confidential?	
What recourse do I have if I disagree with an evaluation?	
How will I use the observation reports to grow and improve my teaching?	

After Three Survey

It is time to reflect back on the past six seminars and what you have accomplished during that time. Spend a few minutes and answer the following questions in the graphic organizer. Your input will help the development of the *Ready for Anything* program and assist the organizers in supplying what is needed for your professional growth.

What should I know and be able to do?

How do I know if I'm being successful?

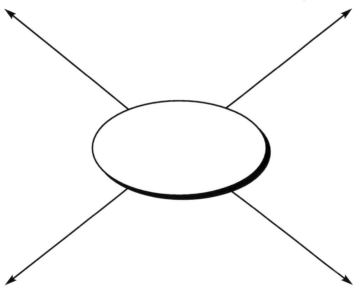

What has helped me develop professionally?

How can we improve our learning during the Ready for Anything *process?*

Seminar Stress Management

Contents

SOME DAYS IT JUST DOESN'T PAY TO GET UP and go to work. Tuesday was one of those days. It was hot and the humidity was thick enough to cut with a knife. The roof in the room had leaked, again, and the maintenance people had come, again, without noticeable improvement—they only came on sunny days, not days like today with its torrential downpours. It was early, and I had just walked into the room, but some of our "before the sun rises" buses had already delivered their first loads of students. My door was open, so Jason quietly entered the room. He said that he had found something in his locker and, knowing how much I liked science, had brought the "something" to me as a present. As I turned around, I saw Jason holding a seven-inch-long snake in his hands. Pleased that he would think so fondly of me, I went and got a large jar and placed the snake inside it. Jason was curious about what kind of snake he'd found. I calmly looked at him and said, "Copperhead."

Introduction

Goal To provide tips, ideas, suggestions, and logistical support to better deal with the day-to-day stress of classroom and school demands

Time frame Two hours

Agenda

Welcome Back and Success Stories; Concerns and Questions

Discussion of INTASC Standard 9: Reflective Practice: Professional Development

Seminar 7: Stress Management

Facilitator Strategies

Teacher-Directed Student Activities

Seminar 7 Reflections

"I'm Ready for Anything" Self-Assessment

TEACHING IS A STRESSFUL JOB. As a new educator, you should expect to experience a certain amount of anxiety during the year, due to the numerous roles and responsibilities you will have to take on. Many stressors are intrinsic to the nature of teaching, and some are beyond our control, such as funding, district mandates, and personnel issues. Teaching is an exhausting, full-time job that requires energy and commitment.

Overview

Beginning teachers state that the second most common stressor is classroom discipline (the first is fear of evaluation). Being taught what to do and how to do the job, *before* they need the information, greatly reduces teachers' stress. This seminar provides multiple strategies and activities for management, organization, and instruction. All of them will help relax and comfort new teachers as they develop into qualified educators.

Preparation

Materials Reproducibles (*figures 7.3–7.7*), sticky notes, basket of toys (such as bubbles, tops, koosh balls, soft darts, etc.), helium-quality balloons, funnels, fine-grained sand or kitty litter, juggling equipment (plastic trash bags, scarves, feathers, balls, clubs, etc.), small white cloths (one per person), waterproof markers, refreshments, door prizes, Special Request form

TODAY'S SEMINAR FOCUSES on strategies that help alleviate the stress created by school and classroom activities. You will help your new teachers understand stress, identify causes of stress, and learn to manage their stress by understanding the demands placed on them. You will need copies of the following:

- Invitation (*figure 7.1*)
- INTASC Standard 9: Reflective Practice: Professional Development (*see figure A*)
- Seminar 7 Overview (*figure 7.2*)
- Reproducibles for facilitator strategies (*figures 7.3 and 7.4*)
- Reproducibles for teacher-directed student activities (*figure 7.5*)
- Seminar 7 Reflections (*figure 7.6*)
- "I'm Ready for Anything" Self-Assessment (*figure 7.7*)
- Special Request form (*figure D*)

Tip

A teacher's response to a perceived crisis determines the level of chaos or calmness that results in a solution. Dealing with a spontaneous event requires on-the-spot thinking—and for a first-year teacher, every challenging situation is a potential crisis. Take time to talk about probable issues and dilemmas that might occur within the classroom setting and discuss ideas and suggestions for dealing with each.

Facilitator Strategies

Focus Identifying your stress areas.

How to Use Use the following strategies to help teachers learn what stresses them the most, and become conscious of the signals of stress.

ABCs of School Stress

Give each participant an ABC grid (*figure 7.3*). Conduct a brainstorming session to identify stress-related and stress-inducing items in the world of new-teacher responsibilities. Insert each item in the grid under the corresponding letter of the alphabet. Take time to evaluate each item, determining which are within the teacher's control and which cannot be controlled. Share stress-reduction solutions and ideas.

Identifying My Stress Points

Give each participant a teacher stress survey (*figure 7.4*) and allow time for them to fill it out. Share responses according to the needs of participants.

Managing the To-Do List

Have participants create a three-column to-do worksheet, using the column headings "Must Do," "Maybe Do," and "Later Do." Write task items on sticky notes and place them in the appropriate column.

It's Play Time

Allow time for participants to play with and enjoy the bucket of toys. Reinforce the idea that "down" time is important!

Stress Balls

Give each person a balloon and time to create a stress ball. Use a funnel and fine-grained sand or cat litter to fill the balloon. Take the balls back to the classroom and use them frequently.

Juggling Is Fun

Arrange time for participants to learn to juggle, using plastic trash bags stuffed with paper, scarves, feathers, balls, or other appropriate practice equipment. If you are not an expert juggler, find someone in your school or community to help with this. Teachers will probably point out that this activity makes physical their juggling of the many and varied demands placed on them every day.

Teacher-Directed Student Activities

Focus Learning to design and ask effective questions.

How Am I Doing?

Select a class and give each student a set of "How Am I Doing?" survey questions (*figure 7.5*). Have students answer the questions and return the surveys for discussion and reflection at the next seminar.

Read Aloud

Reading aloud to students certainly improves reading skills, but it is also a relaxing and enjoyable strategy for classroom use. Select a high-interest text and spend time reading to your class.

Quiet Time

Every now and then, allow several moments of quiet reflection time during the students' stressful day. Play a variety of relaxing music selections while students close their eyes and rest. If you wish to share a motivational thought before Quiet Time, select a saying that will have meaning to the students.

Seminar 7 Reflections

Activity: The Anxiety Towel

Each participant gets a white cloth and a set of permanent markers. Write concerns, issues, problems, and comments on the cloth. Complete the activity by networking solutions to the problems and following up on the comments. Then have each participant "wring out" the problems by wringing the towel vigorously. Keep the towels on hand for future use; over time, the concerns and issues will be washed away with use and the passage of time. *See figure 7.6.*

"I'm Ready for Anything" Self-Assessment (Seminar 7)

See figure 7.7.

Tip

Remind new teachers not to take on too many additional tasks just because they are new and want to impress others. Nothing is more important than personal health and well-being. Your new teachers are a valuable asset to your school, but they can be effective only when they are in their classrooms!

You Are Invited!

Seminar 7: Stress Management

You Are Appreciated!

Date
_____

Time
_____

Location
_____

Nothing in the world can take the place of persistence.

—Calvin Coolidge

Reflections

- What strategies are you using to deal with school-related stress?
- What really irritates you about teaching?

INTASC Standard 9: Reflective Practice: Professional Development

The teacher is a reflective practitioner who continually evaluates the effects of his or her choices and actions on others [students, parents, and other professionals in the learning community] and who actively seeks out opportunities to grow professionally.

Overview

Seminar 7: Stress Management

Goal

To provide tips, ideas, suggestions, and logistical support to better deal with the day-to-day stress of classroom and school demands.

Focus

Today's seminar focuses on strategies that help alleviate stress related to school and classroom activities.

Agenda

Welcome Back and Success Stories; Concerns and Questions

Discussion of INTASC Standard 9: Reflective Practice: Professional Development

Seminar 7: Stress Management

- Facilitator Strategies
  - □ ABCs of School Stress
  - □ Identifying My Stress Points
  - □ Managing the To-Do List

Agenda (Continued)

  - □ It's Play Time
  - □ Stress Balls
  - □ Juggling Is Fun

- Teacher-Directed Student Activities
  - □ How Am I Doing?
  - □ Read Aloud
  - □ Quiet Time

Seminar 7 Reflections

"I'm Ready for Anything" Self-Assessment

INTASC Standard 9: Reflective Practice: Professional Development

The teacher is a reflective practitioner who continually evaluates the effects of his or her choices and actions on others [students, parents, and other professionals in the learning community] and who actively seeks out opportunities to grow professionally.

The ABCs of School Stress

A	B	C	D	E	F
G	H	I	J	K	L
M	N	O	P	Q	R
S	T	U	V	W	X
Y	Z				

Identifying My Stress Points

Place a check in the yes or no column for each item.

	Yes	No
Do you associate with people whose company you enjoy and who support you?	❏	❏
Do you get up early to prepare for the day's lesson?	❏	❏
Do you use the "parking lot" planning method?	❏	❏
Do you use humor in stressful situations?	❏	❏
Do you spend time complaining to colleagues and friends?	❏	❏
Do you have multiple "To Do" notes and lists?	❏	❏
Do you lose materials or supplies because of lack of organization?	❏	❏
Do you arrive late for meetings?	❏	❏
Do you strive to handle each piece of paper only once?	❏	❏
Do you use vacation and weekend days to catch up?	❏	❏
Do you set priorities for each day?	❏	❏
Do you ask questions and get help when needed?	❏	❏
Do you maintain a reasonable diet and sleep habits?	❏	❏
Do you always have to be right?	❏	❏
Do you consistently feel tired or fatigued?	❏	❏
Do you worry about being observed or visited in class?	❏	❏

Name _____

Date _____

"How Am I Doing?" Student Survey

Please answer the following questions by placing a check in the appropriate column.

Your honest and sincere responses are appreciated. I will use your comments to improve my teaching skills and work in this class. This will not affect your grade.

	Yes	No
The teacher is a pleasant person.	❏	❏
The teacher is prepared for class.	❏	❏
The teacher is willing to help me when I need it.	❏	❏
The teacher knows the content and what to teach.	❏	❏
The teacher is enthusiastic.	❏	❏
The teacher has a sense of humor.	❏	❏
The teacher gives good directions.	❏	❏
The teacher's discipline and rules are fair.	❏	❏
The classroom is neat and well organized.	❏	❏
The teacher uses many different teaching ideas.	❏	❏
The teacher gives fair tests.	❏	❏
The teacher encourages me to take responsibility for my learning.	❏	❏
The teacher is always welcoming and respectful to me.	❏	❏
The teacher enjoys working with us.	❏	❏

Seminar 7 Reflections

Activity: The Anxiety Towel

You have a white cloth and permanent, colored markers.

Decorate your cloth with concerns, issues, and problems that you have

or are experiencing this year. "Wring out" the cloth and use it as a reminder

that you can solve problems and wash them away.

INTASC Standard 9: Reflective Practice: Professional Development

The teacher is a reflective practitioner who continually evaluates the effects

of his or her choices and actions on others [students, parents, and other

professionals in the learning community] and who actively seeks

out opportunities to grow professionally.

Self-Assessment

"I'm Ready for Anything" Self-Assessment (Seminar 7)

How Am I Doing?	Personal Comments
How do my lessons reflect planning and organization?	
How well do I handle deadlines?	
What do I do to prepare for parent conferences?	
How do I deal with observations by the administrative team?	
Do I have a plan for keeping up with paperwork?	
Where and how up-to-date is my to-do list? *How many lists do I have?*	
Do I take time for my family and friends?	
What kind of hobbies or fun activities do I continue?	
How do I find the time to talk to my mentor and colleagues?	
Am I late to school and early to leave? *Do I use the "parking lot" method of planning?*	
How do I use my teacher workdays and vacation days?	
What is my fitness routine?	
Do I perceive myself as a perfectionist? *Do I take things personally?*	
Do I worry about the next day?	

Seminar (8) Effective Questioning

Contents

I DEVELOPED "WHERE AM I?": It was the best game, and it lasted a whole year. Each week of the school year, students were asked to solve a geography puzzle with only a small picture, a tiny map section, and a nebulous clue. The first weeks were easy, using such places as the White House, the Statue of Liberty, and the Grand Canyon. As the year progressed, the game became much more difficult and the competition for points increased with each week. The student who solved the most puzzles was to get a steak dinner courtesy of me.

With only two weeks to go in the year, Ben had not missed a single location. Ben's dad came in and played each week, but vowed that he was competing against his son and not providing help. The class was rooting for Ben, and betting that I couldn't make a puzzle hard enough to stump him. When the last week came, the clue on Monday said, "Strikes a match." On Tuesday, a map section with a line representing a road and the number "57" was shown. The picture, which came on Wednesday, represented a rolling expanse of grassland and hills.

Everyone at school got involved. The principal wished me luck on the morning announcements; students posted signs around the school in support of Ben. Finally, Thursday—the final day—arrived, and Ben filled out his "Where Am I?" answer form. Tension mounted as I read his answer: "Flint Hills, Kansas." I took Ben, and his dad, for a wonderful dinner.

The rest of the story? Ben had sat for two nights poring over the Rand McNally atlas until he found that section of road. He then

Introduction

Goal To provide tips, ideas, suggestions, and activities to extend student thinking through effective questioning

Time frame Two hours

Agenda

Welcome Back and Success Stories; Concerns and Questions

Discussion of INTASC Standard 4: Multiple Instructional Strategies

Seminar 8: Effective Questioning

Facilitator Strategies

Teacher-Directed Student Activities

Seminar 8 Reflections

"I'm Ready for Anything" Self-Assessment

called the closest Chamber of Commerce, described the clue and the picture, and was immediately told the answer. The man he spoke to on the phone wanted to meet this unique and creative teacher who had so challenged this young student!

THERE IS NO DOUBT THAT IF WE IMPROVE

teacher questioning skills, we will improve student thinking skills. Good questions should introduce the lesson, expand on the content, and review for comprehension and understanding. Effective questions encourage students to participate in the lesson, develop critical and creative thinking skills, and become more productive test takers. Research reveals that 80 percent to 90 percent of the questions asked in classrooms are at the lowest cognitive level; we also know that learning to ask good questions is a process that develops over time and with practice.

To help beginning teachers develop their questioning skills, this seminar incorporates Bloom's Taxonomy of Cognitive Development, along with strategies that form a strong, easy-to-use foundation for learning effective questioning. In 1956, Benjamin Bloom developed a classification of levels of intellectual behavior that are important to learning. His taxonomy provides teachers with a structure for developing and categorizing questions. We chose this model for inclusion in the seminar because it is widely accepted; has six levels of questions, ranging from easy to thought-provoking; and is appropriate to use with students with identified exceptionalities.

Anderson and Krathwohl (2001) revised Bloom's original taxonomy by combining the cognitive process with the knowledge components. The revised levels of thinking are: remember, understand, apply, analyze, evaluate, and create. Robert Marzano, in *Dimensions of Thinking: A Framework for Curriculum and Instruction* (1998), also addressed levels of thinking, a concept that is widely accepted and used in state test development.

Overview

This seminar provides practice in developing and learning to ask a variety of levels of questions during class. Strategies and activities are included for teacher reflection and student work time. Several models of thinking are discussed, but the facilitator has the final decision on which will best suit the needs of individual participants and students.

Preparation

Materials Reproducibles (*figures 8.3–8.12*), card stock, scissors, copier, laminator, paper clips, refreshments, door prizes, Special Request form

TODAY'S SEMINAR FOCUSES on the implementation of effective questioning in the classroom through teacher and student strategies. You will need copies of the following:

- Invitation (*figure 8.1*)
- INTASC Standard 4: Multiple Instructional Strategies (*see figure A*)
- Seminar 8 Overview (*figure 8.2*)
- Reproducibles for facilitator strategies (*figures 8.3 and 8.4*)
- Reproducibles for teacher-directed student activities (*figures 8.5–8.10*)
- Seminar 8 Reflections (*figure 8.11*)
- "I'm Ready for Anything" Self-Assessment (*figure 8.12*)
- Special Request form (*figure D*)

Tip

It is through questioning that students develop problem-solving skills and divergent thinking. Take time to practice developing multiple levels of questions to use with review, teacher input, and assessment. Make sure that lesson plans contain questions that are appropriately challenging for all levels of academic ability, and that teachers practice Wait Time I and II.

Tip

Give *everyone* a door prize!

Facilitator Strategies

Focus Implementing effective questioning in the daily lesson plan.

How to Use Use the following strategies to help teachers improve the effectiveness of and variety of levels in their questioning.

Questioning Checklist

Begin the session with a discussion of the questioning checklist. *See figure 8.3.*

Wait Time I and II

Discuss the importance of wait time. Practice pausing one to two seconds after asking a question and before calling on a student. Also, pause one to two seconds before affirming a student response.

Questions with Bloom

Take time to talk about the importance of learning to develop and ask good questions. Spend time during the seminar to review and practice writing questions according to Bloom's Taxonomy of Cognitive Development. Help your new teachers with the teacher-directed student activities and effective question design. *See figure 8.4.*

Teacher-Directed Student Activities

Focus Learning to design and ask effective questions.

Questioning Word of the Day

Provide students with key terms and phrases found in the end-of-grade question stems. All of the multiple-choice questions on standardized tests contain vocabulary and questions that ask the reader to analyze the answers carefully. By helping students understand the words and what the question is asking, you help students develop improved test-taking skills and answering capacity. *Figure 8.5* provides a sample list of key terms and question stems; students should become familiar with their meanings and levels of thinking. Creating a classroom testing word wall or vocabulary journal (with the term, its definition, an illustration, and an example) helps to supplement this learning.

Questioning Taxonomy

The questioning taxonomy is a tool for improving the levels of thinking of and question generation by both teachers and students. The graphic (*figure 8.6*) provides examples of thinking verbs found in Bloom's Taxonomy. Teachers may use this figure as a "cheat sheet" for their own use, distribute copies for student use in their notebooks, or enlarge it as a classroom display. If used as a transparency, it becomes a questioning wheel (*figure 8.7*) for in-class discussion. The facilitator who models this activity should provide a copy of a questioning taxonomy and transparency for use in classrooms and give each participant the opportunity to create and design a customized display for his or her classroom.

Questioning Cubes and Wheels

The facilitator should allow time for participants to make questioning cubes (*figure 8.8*) out of cardstock, for use in the classroom during small-group work. Create enough cubes for each group of students. Use the cubes, as you work with individual groups, to randomly "roll" a thinking-verb category. Create a question at that level of thinking and present it to the group for discussion. For example, a roll of "Comprehension" could stimulate creation of a question beginning with *describe, give examples, illustrate,* or *explain.*

Tip

Make sure that your lesson plans contain the questions you will ask during class. Take time to write out the questions. Your instructional presentation will move more smoothly if you have prepared your discussions in advance.

During the seminar, the facilitator will allow time for you to make questioning wheels (*figure 8.7*) for use in teacher-directed questioning in class. Make a transparency of the wheel and use a paper clip, in the center, to spin for selection of question verbs for review and discussion. You may also make enough question wheels (out of cardstock) for students to independently create their own questions during small-group work and discussion.

Questioning Organizers

A questioning organizer is a wonderful tool for giving notes and information to students or as an independent activity for students. Teachers should provide instruction that requires an incremental thinking process. The facilitator will give each participant a questioning organizer (*figure 8.9*) and transparency to use in the classroom. You will have time to create examples of the six levels of questions specifically related to the content that you are teaching.

The organizer is designed to correspond to the six levels of thinking (the number of sides in the graphic increase as the complexity of the thinking level increases). Using the Questioning Taxonomy (*see figure 8.6*) to choose appropriate verbs from each level, write words into the shapes on the organizer. For example, write the content topic in the middle of the graphic and a selected thinking verb in each of the shapes.

Example: circle = *define,* triangle = *give examples,* square = *use,* pentagon = *compare,* and so forth. Notes or answers should be written next to the shapes for students to review and discuss.

Beginning a Unit with Focused Questions

Use this strategy to begin a unit. Students will generate their own questions around the topics on the graphic organizer. *See figure 8.10.* The facilitator will give each participant a copy of the "Beginning a Unit" graphic organizer and transparency to use for giving notes and content.

Questioning Journal

Give each student the opportunity to design and develop a personal journal, using question stems, key terms and phrases, tips and thoughts, study skill support ideas, and motivational quotes and comments.

Seminar 8 Reflections

Activity: The Web of Questions

Use a six-sided graphic to visually illustrate the six levels of thinking skills as related to new-teacher issues and concerns. Follow up with a discussion after allowing individual time to focus on each question and answer.

Suggested verbs include: *tell, describe, model, draw conclusions, create, evaluate. See figure 8.11.*

"I'm Ready for Anything" Self-Assessment (Seminar 8)

See figure 8.12.

Tip

Although you are always questioning the students, take time to ask yourself, "How am I doing?" and "What have I done well?"

You Are Invited!

Seminar 8: Effective Questioning

Good teaching is about: passion, doing your best, style, humor, relationships, respect, flexibility, a need for support, and the kids.

Date
_____

Time
_____

Location
_____

It is not the answer that enlightens, but the question.

—Eugene Ionesco

Reflections

- What type of questions do you ask, and how do you know?

- What makes your best lessons work? What are the most challenging components?

INTASC Standard 4: Multiple Instructional Strategies

The teacher understands and uses a variety of instructional strategies to encourage student development of critical thinking, problem solving, and performance skills.

Overview

Seminar 8: Effective Questioning

Goal

To provide tips, ideas, suggestions, and activities to extend student thinking through effective questioning.

Focus

Today's seminar focuses on the implementation of effective questioning in the classroom through teacher and student strategies.

Agenda

Welcome Back and Success Stories; Concerns and Questions

Discussion of INTASC Standard 4: Multiple Instructional Strategies

Seminar 8: Effective Questioning

- Facilitator Strategies
  - □ Questioning Checklist
  - □ Wait Time I and II
  - □ Questions with Bloom

Agenda *(Continued)*

- Teacher-Directed Student Activities
  - □ Questioning Word of the Day
  - □ Questioning Taxonomy
  - □ Questioning Cubes and Wheels
  - □ Questioning Organizers
  - □ Beginning a Unit with Focused Questions
  - □ Questioning Journal

Seminar 8 Reflections

"I'm Ready for Anything" Self-Assessment

INTASC Standard 4: Multiple Instructional Strategies

The teacher understands and uses a variety of instructional strategies to encourage student development of critical thinking, problem solving, and performance skills.

Questioning Checklist

Question	Reflection
❏ Do I regularly plan to ask all levels of questions?	
❏ Do my lesson plans reflect effective questioning?	
❏ Do I use my "hint sheets" to implement questioning?	
❏ Do I access prior knowledge before beginning a lesson?	
❏ Do I practice Wait Time I and II?	
❏ Do I allow students to create their own questions?	
❏ Do I allow students to summarize and reflect within the class period?	
❏ Do I visually survey my class for correct responses?	
❏ Do I model "thinking out loud" as a regular process?	
❏ Do I ask questions at progressively higher levels of thinking?	
❏ Do I use visuals to stimulate questioning?	

Bloom's Taxonomy of Cognitive Development

Bloom's Taxonomy is a series of six levels of cognitive thinking. It is important to work through each of the six levels as you review, provide content input, and assess learning. Begin your question with the verb and end with the content listed in your curriculum materials. A revision of the thinking categories, which was completed in 2001, is represented by the italicized terms next to the originals.

KNOWLEDGE/*Remember* (K)

Questions at this level ask students to recall and remember information

Question Cues ————————→ list, match, name, label, tell, define, memorize, draw, identify

COMPREHENSION/*Understand* (C)

Questions at this level ask students to understand and interpret information

Question cues ————————→ describe, illustrate, give examples, change, retell, restate, explain in your own words, summarize, how could

APPLICATION/*Apply* (AP)

Questions at this level ask students to use information to solve problems in new situations

Question cues ————————→ determine, save, what other, apply, interpret, use, model, choose, teach, make

ANALYSIS/*Analyze* (AN)

Questions at this level ask students to see patterns and organize information

Question cues ————————→ compare, research, contrast, investigate, draw conclusions, tell why, demonstrate, show

SYNTHESIS/*Evaluate* (SY)

Questions at this level ask students to use previous knowledge to create new ideas or products

Question cues ————————→ create, improve, design, construct, invent, plan, determine, organize, classify, predict

EVALUATION/*Create* (EV)

Questions at this level ask students to assess or justify the value of information

Question cues ————————→ defend, consider, justify, rate, evaluate, select, support, recommend, in your opinion, agree, disagree

End-of-Year Key Questioning Terms and Question Stems

Questioning Terms

A

affect
all
always
analyze
apply
assume

B

best

C

choose
clarify
compare
construct
contrast
convey

D

define
describe
discriminate
discuss

E

effect
elaborate
evaluate
explain

G

generate

I

identify
infer
influence

J

justify

L

list
locate

M

maybe

O

often
organize

P

predict

R

react
reference
represent

S

seldom
select
solve
summarize

Question Stems

What is the best . . .

Which of the following . . .

The author's purpose . . .

Which is most *likely to . . .*

What is the main purpose . . .

According to the author . . .

Find the significance of . . .

What can you expect to read . . .

In the passage . . .

What is the main idea . . .

Why does the narrator . . .

What type of text . . .

This text is an example of . . .

What idea can you get . . .

Which of the following best *summarizes . . .*

How would you summarize the main idea . . .

Which list of numbers . . .

How much . . .

How many . . .

What is the total . . .

Determine least to greatest . . .

Questioning Taxonomy

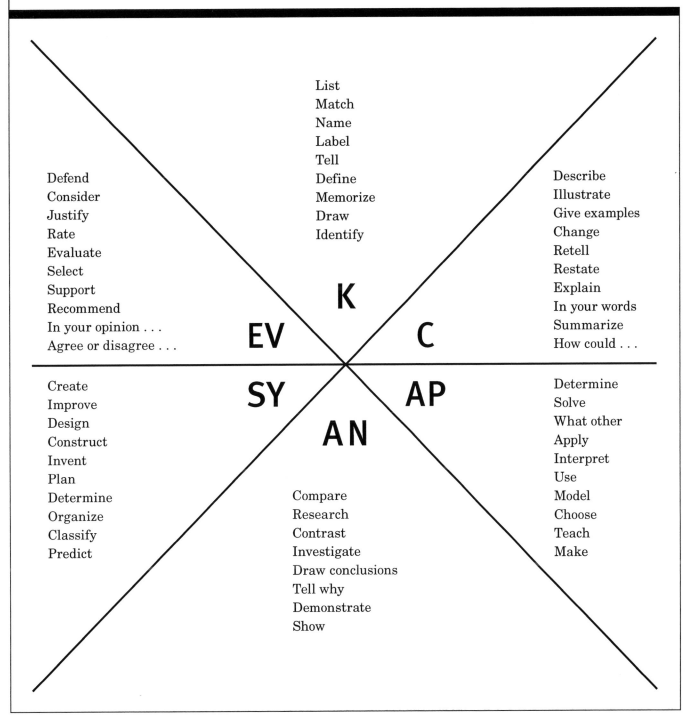

List
Match
Name
Label
Tell
Define
Memorize
Draw
Identify

K

Defend
Consider
Justify
Rate
Evaluate
Select
Support
Recommend
In your opinion . . .
Agree or disagree . . .

EV

Describe
Illustrate
Give examples
Change
Retell
Restate
Explain
In your words
Summarize
How could . . .

C

Create
Improve
Design
Construct
Invent
Plan
Determine
Organize
Classify
Predict

SY

AP

AN

Compare
Research
Contrast
Investigate
Draw conclusions
Tell why
Demonstrate
Show

Determine
Solve
What other
Apply
Interpret
Use
Model
Choose
Teach
Make

Questioning Wheels

Q
U
E
S
T
I
O
N
I
N
G

W
H
E
E
L
S

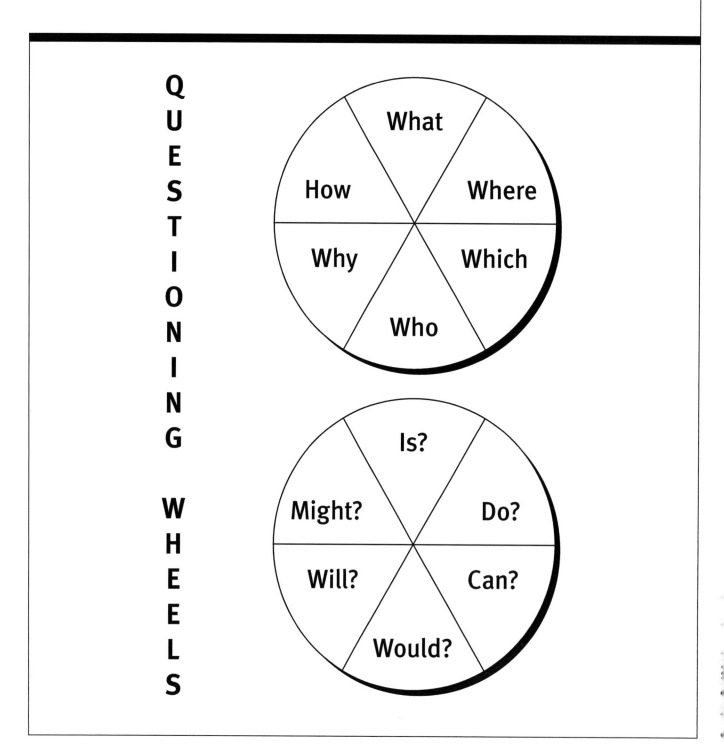

Questioning Cube

Knowledge

Comprehension | Application

Analysis | Synthesis

Evaluation

Questioning Graphic Organizer

Taxonomy of Questioning

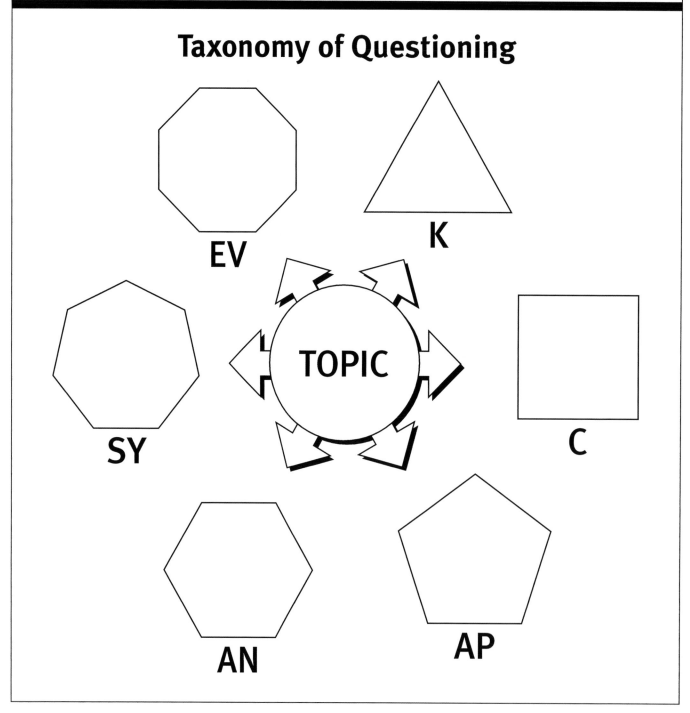

Beginning a Unit with Focused Questions

Beginning a Unit

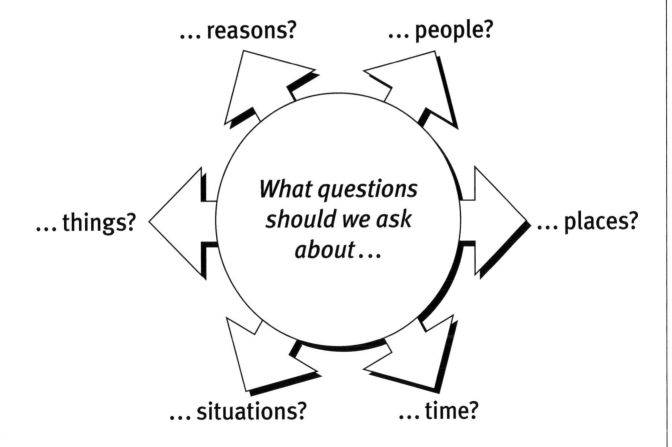

... reasons?

... people?

... things?

What questions should we ask about...

... places?

... situations?

... time?

Seminar 8 Reflections

Activity: The Web of Questions

Use the six-sided graphic to visually illustrate
the six levels of thinking skills as related to new-teacher
issues and concerns. Follow up with a discussion after teachers
have had time to focus on each question and answer.

Suggested verbs include: *tell, describe, model, draw conclusions, create, evaluate.*

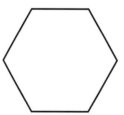

INTASC Standard 4: Multiple Instructional Strategies

The teacher understands and uses a variety of instructional
strategies to encourage student development of
critical thinking, problem solving, and
performance skills.

Self-Assessment

"I'm Ready for Anything" Self-Assessment (Seminar 8)

How Am I Doing?	Personal Comments
Do I plan my questions before class?	
Where in my lesson plans is a list of questions related to the content of the day?	
What kind of self-help hint sheets do I use in class to remind me to ask better questions?	
How have I implemented Wait Time I & II?	
Have I given my students a list of the taxonomy verbs and question stems? *Have I taught them to use these items?*	
What does my questioning wall look like?	
How did I begin a recent unit with student-developed questions?	
How have we used questioning wheels and cubes?	
What does my questioning taxonomy bulletin board look like?	
Have I given my students questioning bookmarks to use at home?	
Who have I had in my classroom to observe my questioning skills? Did I use a video or audio method?	
What kind of homework have I given to support effective questioning?	

Seminar 9 The Test

Contents

I MET A VERY PRECOCIOUS FOURTH-GRADER who was rather bored with all the testing programs. He asked me if I knew the superintendent and whether I would be willing to share something about testing with him. After I assured this boy that his identity would be kept confidential, he told me that if he saw any more "Test Up, Test Down, Test Prep, Test Now, Test Then" materials, he would "Screw Up, Screw Down, Screw Now, and Screw Then" the test.

I really understood his frustration; looking around his teacher's room, I saw no fewer than 20 different kinds of testing workbooks and materials. He and I finally decided that because I also had the responsibility of monitoring summer school, and I really didn't want to see him there, he would do his best to pass his part of the test.

WE HAVE BECOME A NATION OF TESTS, testers, and testing. Though we don't profess to "teach to the test," we do a tremendous amount of test-taking preparation. Weeks before state testing begins, schools start to pump up school spirit and enthusiasm for the reading, writing, and math tests. Posters, pep rallies, slogan contests, skits, and word-of-the-day quizzes take priority over all other instruction in the school. Remediation and acceleration groups spring up like weeds, and students are moved from teacher to teacher for "just one more review" of an objective.

Introduction

Goal To provide tips, ideas, suggestions, and logistical support to help students understand and implement the best strategies for successful test taking.

Time frame Two hours

Agenda

Welcome Back and Success Stories; Concerns and Questions

Discussion of INTASC Standard 8: Assessment

Seminar 9: The Test

Facilitator Strategy

Teacher-Directed Student Activities

Seminar 9 Reflections

"I'm Ready for Anything" Self-Assessment

After Three Survey

Overview

This seminar allows the facilitator to discuss the testing program and offers activities through which students can improve their test-taking skills. Many state tests include multiple-choice, short-answer, and extended-response types of questions, and teachers should be aware of the thought processes required to answer each. Help teachers realize that testing creates various levels of anxiety in administrators, staff, and students, and that those responses vary during the testing period. Provide teacher-directed activities to help students become successful test takers.

Preparation

Materials State and local testing code of ethics and procedures; reproducibles (*figures 9.3–9.6*); small pieces of poster board; markers; sample photos for projecting and modeling the P.O.A. method; lists of test-related terms, phrases, and question stems; *After Three* survey; refreshments; door prizes; Special Request form

TODAY'S SEMINAR PROVIDES an understanding of the end-of-year test and classroom strategies for improving students' skills for testing. You will need copies of the following:

- An invitation (*figure 9.1*)
- INTASC Standard 8: Assessment (*see figure A*)
- Seminar 9 Overview (*figure 9.2*)
- Reproducible (*figure 9.3*)
- Seminar 9 Reflections (*figure 9.4*)
- "I'm Ready for Anything" Self-Assessment (*figure 9.5*)
- *After Three* Survey (*figure 9.6*)
- Special Request form (*figure D*)

Tip

Make sure that your new teachers understand the logistics, format, and content of the state and district testing programs.

Tip

Provide some really
great refreshments for this
seminar!

Facilitator Strategy

Focus Understanding the test and test-taking strategies.

How to Use Use the following strategy to help teachers
understand the law, the tests (format and content), and the
student skills needed for successful test taking.

Understanding the Law and the Test

Provide new teachers with information specific to state and
local testing procedures and protocols. This session should tell
them everything they need to know about the end-of-year tests,
including applicable laws and regulations, protocols, ethics,
test format, test content, and so on.

Teacher-Directed Student Activities

Focus Helping students to become more proficient test takers.

I See Myself

Allow students to produce a motivational poster, skit, slogan,
or broadcast on "Getting Ready for the Test." Share and award
recognition for each presentation.

T.I.P.

Teach students to recognize the following three components of
analysis of a nonfiction text:

T = Title

I = Introductory sentence or paragraph and what it predicts
about the text

P = Preview any key terms (bold, italics, or underlined in the
text) and determine what each means

Multiple Media Sources

Expose students to multiple types of text media, including recipes, graphs and charts, advertisements, maps, brochures, poems, letters, and editorials.

Whisper Reading

Many state tests include lengthy reading passages that test student stamina and endurance. Practice reading nonfiction text aloud in a whisper tone for a set amount of time. Begin with short intervals and build up to five minutes of sustained whisper reading.

The Line Stops Here

Practice identifying the main idea, key vocabulary, and graphics that are central to an understanding of text content. Have students overlay a transparency page on the text and use markers to locate each of these items, using a square for the main idea, triangles for vocabulary, and circles for charts, graphs, or maps. Take time to share student work with the class.

The P.O.A. Method

This activity helps students focus on the numerous visual elements found in end-of-grade tests. Locate a series of photographs, graphics, and/or illustrations that relate to the content. Show them as visuals and have students analyze the images. Use the P.O.A. method to discuss how each image relates to the subject matter; the following are suggested starter questions:

P = **People**—Are there people in the image? Who are they? What is their role in the image?

O = **Objects**—Are there objects in the image? If so, how do they support the people?

A = **Action**—Is there action in the image? How does this relate to understanding the image?

Tip

Make sure to find out if students are allowed to mark in the state testing documents.

Tip

Encourage students to think of the test as an opportunity to show off what they have learned throughout the year. It is a chance for them to brag and celebrate.

The Testing Bookmark

Provide each student with a testing bookmark (*figure 9.3*) listing test-taking tips and strategies.

Words, Words, Words

Create a word wall with key terms, phrases, and question stems from or related to the end-of-grade test format. Practice using the words every day so that students become familiar with the meanings of the words and know how to use the terms, phrases, and question stems in a test context.

The Top Ten List

Ten days before the end-of-year test, post and discuss a test-taking tip of the day. Sample tips include:

- Take time to skim the test first
- Read all directions and test questions carefully
- Use the process of elimination
- Go back and review your answers if you finish early
- Get plenty of rest the night before and eat a good breakfast
- Look for and analyze the question stem
- Use all your test time
- Bring your materials and be prepared
- Recheck all your math computations
- Do not give up!

Seminar 9 Reflections

Activity: The Billboard

Arrange teachers around tables in groups of three to four. Brainstorm a list of good test-taking strategies and tips. Have each group create a group poster displaying ideas, tips, and suggestions to help students improve their test-taking skills. Use these posters as models and let each teacher's class create their own, or place these posters around the school as a display. *See figure 9.4.*

"I'm Ready for Anything" Self-Assessment (Seminar 9)

See figure 9.5.

After Three Survey

Give participants time to complete the *After Three* survey (*figure 9.6*). Use the responses for review of and revisions to the *Ready for Anything* program, as appropriate.

Quote

I'm always ready to learn, but I do not always like being taught.

—Sir Winston Churchill

You Are Invited!

Seminar 9: The Test

*I have almost made it! I have almost made it! I can't believe
I made it a year! I am so proud of myself! Look what I
know now that I didn't know when I started!*

Date
_____

Time
_____

Location
_____

Reflections

- Why do you need to know the testing code of ethics?

- What will I do differently next year?

INTASC Standard 8: Assessment

The teacher understands and uses formal and informal assessment strategies to
evaluate and ensure the continuous intellectual, social, and physical development of
the learner.

Overview

Seminar 9: The Test

Goal

To provide tips, ideas, suggestions, and logistical support to understand and implement the best strategies for successful test taking.

Focus

Today's seminar provides an understanding of the end-of-year test and classroom strategies for improving student skills for testing.

Agenda

Welcome Back and Success Stories; Concerns and Questions

Discussion of INTASC Standard 8: Assessment

Seminar 9: The Test

■ Facilitator Strategy

  □ Understanding the Law and the Test

Agenda *(Continued)*

■ Teacher-Directed Student Activities

  □ I See Myself

  □ T.I.P.

  □ Multiple Media Sources

  □ Whisper Reading

  □ The Line Stops Here

  □ The P.O.A. Method

  □ The Testing Bookmark

  □ Word, Words, Words

  □ The Top Ten List

Seminar 9 Reflections

"I'm Ready for Anything" Self-Assessment

After Three Survey

INTASC Standard 8: Assessment

The teacher understands and uses formal and informal assessment strategies to evaluate and ensure continuous intellectual, social, and physical development of the learner.

Student Testing Bookmark

Suggestions for Test Takers

- Be prepared
- Eat a good breakfast
- Have your materials ready
- Get a good night's rest
- Dress comfortably
- Have a positive attitude

Some Questions to Remember

- *Which of the following . . . ?*
- *What is the best . . . ?*
- *Based on the passage . . .*
- *What is the main idea . . . ?*
- *According to the author . . .*
- *What is the most likely . . . ?*
- *What is the most important . . . ?*
- *What caused . . . ?*
- *What might the author mean . . . ?*
- *What is the purpose . . . ?*

Test-Taking Strategies

- Read the questions before the passage
- Look for key question stems
- Look for bold, italicized, or underlined words
- Ignore students who finish first
- Make your answer marks carefully
- Remember the different types of text
- Eliminate choices you know are wrong
- Watch your time and pace your work
- Answer the questions you know first
- Take a deep breath every now and then
- Check your answers when you finish
- Recheck your math calculations

Seminar 9 Reflections

Activity: The Billboard

Place yourself in a group of three or four around a table. Brainstorm a list of good test-taking strategies and tips. Use the supplies to create a group poster displaying ideas, tips, and suggestions to help students improve test-taking skills. Use this as a model and have each teacher's class create their own, or place your posters around the school as a display.

INTASC Standard 8: Assessment

The teacher understands and uses formal and informal assessment strategies to evaluate and ensure the continuous intellectual, social, and physical development of the learner.

Self-Assessment

"I'm Ready for Anything" Self-Assessment (Seminar 9)

How Am I Doing?	Personal Comments
What have I learned about the facts of the state test?	
Have I identified individual students' modifications and needs for the test?	
How have I included end-of-grade test question stems in my teaching?	
How have I included roots, prefixes, and suffixes in my teaching?	
Have I presented test-taking skills each day?	
Have I implemented motivational components for success? If so, which ones?	
Does each student understand the complexity of and facts about the test?	
What strategies have I used to support good test taking?	
How does my attitude influence student success?	
Have I been trained on the testing code of ethics?	
What materials do I need to be ready for the day of the test?	
What do I do before, during, and after the test so as not to violate the testing code of ethics?	
How will we celebrate success after the test?	

After Three Survey

It is time to reflect back on the past nine seminars and what has been accomplished during this time. Divide your group into fours and count off one through four. Each person will have an opportunity to network with the people of the same number for approximately 10 minutes. Take time to discuss the question in your numbered group and be ready to return to your original group with comments and discussion items.

Group Number 1   What have been the benefits of the *Ready for Anything* process this year? Cite several examples that have had a significant effect on your teaching skills and knowledge.

Group Number 2   What have been the challenges of being a new teacher? What successes did you experience throughout the year?

Group Number 3   What suggestions do you have for next year's *Ready for Anything* program? What has worked? What would you revise or change?

Group Number 4   Why would you consider returning to this school next year? What has helped or hindered your decision? How could this be changed?

After spending time with your numbered group, return to your original group and share the responses. Take time to share with the facilitator.

If you wish to make additional comments, please do so in writing and give the comment sheet to your facilitator.

Seminar (10) Surviving the Last Weeks of School

Contents

ONE OF MY FAVORITE PRINCIPALS CALLED me about a situation concerning one of her new teachers and a small group of students. The teacher, who had just attended seminar 10, knew that students would celebrate and had planned a complex, integrated unit with 12 different activities for a culmination of the year in social studies. She noticed that a group of six students was particularly loud and boisterous, but thought that it was because *all* students celebrate, or because they were really enjoying the activity.

The group continued to socialize in an extremely animated fashion and did not respond well to her discipline requests for reduced noise. They continued to snack and drink, as allowed in this class, while working on the activity, moving about, giggling, and playing. Finally, the teacher approached the group and gave the ultimatum: *No more talking!* She accidentally knocked over one of their soda bottles and immediately discovered the reason for their ecstatic state of mind: all the drinks contained gin.

Introduction

Goal To provide tips, ideas, suggestions, and activities for successfully ending the school year.

Time frame Two hours

Agenda

Welcome Back and Success Stories; Concerns and Questions

Discussion of INTASC Standard 10: School and Community Involvement

Seminar 10: Surviving the Last Weeks of School

Facilitator Strategies

Teacher-Directed Student Activities

Seminar 10 Reflections

"I'm Ready for Anything" Self-Assessment

PRINCIPALS MANDATE THAT THE LAST TWO weeks of school be academically focused, with no videos used and strong instructional plans in place. The expectation is that teachers will continue with the academic program and maintain a positive, safe learning environment, and that students will follow the rules. We encourage our teachers to tighten the rope, to gear up and be ready to deal with students who are ready to celebrate. Some teachers use this time to implement interdisciplinary, end-of-the-year units, and cooperative groups tend to be the instructional norm. Many times teachers use this time to reinforce additional skills or teach a unit that is of high interest to students. It is a time for endurance and organization along with a high level of anticipation of the end of the year.

Other teachers allow a more relaxed atmosphere and permit students time for snacks and drinks as they work through additional content. Often the district requires teachers to take up textbooks, collect and inventory materials, and begin the closeout process. This typically means that teachers are left to fend for themselves and rely on their ingenuity or the support of other teachers and materials. Planning for the last weeks should occur several months before the end of school. Lessons should be highly structured, with activities and strategies that continue to support the academic programs.

Overview

This seminar provides end-of-year, culminating strategies for working with students during the last few weeks of school. The overarching idea is to maintain an academic focus through the end of the school term, despite the natural tendency to slack off in anticipation of the break.

Preparation

Materials School-based samples of end-of-the year paperwork and forms; reproducibles (*figures 10.3–10.5*); end-of-year grading procedures; school-based procedures for turning in materials and equipment; scrapbook, album, spiral notebook, journal, and/or digital camera, refreshments, door prizes, Special Request form

TODAY'S SEMINAR FOCUSES on strategies and activities for ending the school year. In particular, it helps teachers maintain an academic orientation for the end of the year. You will need copies of the following:

- Invitation (*figure 10.1*)
- INTASC Standard 10: School and Community Involvement (*see figure A*)
- Seminar 10 Overview (*figure 10.2*)
- Reproducible (*figure 10.3*)
- Seminar 10 Reflections (*figure 10.4*)
- "I'm Ready for Anything" Self-Assessment (*figure 10.5*)
- Special Request form (*figure D*)

Tip

Help new teachers understand that everyone will be ready for the end of school and that all students will celebrate. Make sure teachers know that even though materials and equipment may be turned in before the close of school, students must continue to be engaged with activities that support the instructional plan.

Facilitator Strategies

Focus What is expected before the end of school?

How to Use Use the following strategies to help teachers learn and follow the end-of-year procedures, while maintaining an academic orientation in the classroom.

Reams of Paper

Tell your new teachers what paperwork is required before the end of school. This includes showing samples of report cards, summer addresses, attendance cards, grades, cumulative folders, and so on, as appropriate for your school.

Closing Out the Room

All staff members are required to complete the end-of-year tasks and duties. Each school has different procedures for handling equipment and materials, so review the required school checkout list and add or delete items as needed. Take time to explain which items are to be turned in, inventoried and stored, cleaned, and/or taken home. *See figure 10.3.*

Taking Inventory

Share the school procedures for turning in school-based items (e.g., audiovisual equipment, manipulative kits, textbooks, curriculum materials). Make sure teachers know what they are responsible for.

Testing and Grades

Share the procedures for end-of-year testing and determination of grades. Make sure that projects, make-up work, and end-of-year tests are graded, averaged, and recorded.

Tip

Take photos of your new teachers for a special framed memento given at the end of the year.

Teacher-Directed Student Activities

Focus Saying goodbye and good luck to students.

Advice for Next Year

Have your students write letters of advice to next year's class members, telling them what to expect from you and offering suggestions.

Everyone Has a Story to Tell

Have students create a timeline representing the year in your classroom. Include illustrations, creative writing, quotes, and other materials. Share with all.

End-of-the-Year Journal

Allow students to share comments, illustrations, and thoughts to be included in your First-Year Teacher's Journal. Take pictures of each class for your journal—and don't forget to include their names!

Ending Mural

Provide groups of students with large sheets of paper and supplies. Have each group create a graphic organizer or mural of all that was learned in the year.

I Remember When

Divide students into pairs and have them create a list of the Top Ten things they remember best about the year. Share the lists with the class.

Quote

Keep up the pace and don't let up during the last few weeks. Teach to the end, even though everyone is ready for a break, or they will get the upper hand.

—First-year eighth-grade teacher

My Accomplishments

Give each student a piece of paper. Have students divide the paper into four sections. Complete the following in each section, using words and/or illustrations:

1. Your favorite thing about the class
2. What you are the most proud of
3. Several words of advice for the teacher
4. What you are looking forward to next year

Take time to share the responses with the class.

It's About the Knowledge

Think about an area of content that you taught this year and take time to brainstorm vocabulary and key information. Have students create a list with you, on paper. Provide each student with a piece of paper and ask each one to design a large graphic organizer that incorporates what he or she learned during the year.

Seminar 10 Reflections

Activity: The Year in Review

Use the sample list of words to describe and summarize the year (*figure 10.4*). Write each word or phrase on a card and pass the cards out among the participants. Allow time for your new teachers to reflect on these questions:

- What were the most memorable events of the year?
- What events or incidents were the most challenging?
- What did you do well?

Sample words: classroom management, conferences, lesson plans, observations, paperwork, testing, stress, deadlines, climate, building relationships, planning, time management

"I'm Ready for Anything" Self-Assessment (Seminar 10)

See figure 10.5.

You Are Invited!

Seminar 10: Surviving the Last Weeks of School

*It is a proven fact that students will celebrate
long before you want them to.*

Date
_____

Time
_____

Location
_____

You have almost made it!

Reflections

- What was the best part of the year?

INTASC Standard 10: School and Community Involvement

The teacher fosters relationships with school colleagues, parents, and agencies in the
larger community to support students' learning and well-being.

Overview

Seminar 10: Surviving the Last Weeks of School

Goal

To provide tips, ideas, suggestions, and activities for successfully ending the school year.

Focus

Today's seminar focuses on strategies and suggestions for ending the school year.

Agenda

Welcome Back and Success Stories; Concerns and Questions

Discussion of INTASC Standard 10: School and Community Involvement

Seminar 10: Surviving the Last Weeks of School

- Facilitator Strategies
  - □ Reams of Paper
  - □ Closing Out the Room
  - □ Taking Inventory
  - □ Testing and Grades

Agenda *(Continued)*

- Teacher-Directed Student Activities
  - □ Advice for Next Year
  - □ Everyone Has a Story to Tell
  - □ End-of-the-Year Journal
  - □ Ending Mural
  - □ I Remember When
  - □ My Accomplishments
  - □ It's About the Knowledge

Seminar 10 Reflections

"I'm Ready for Anything" Self-Assessment

INTASC Standard 10: School and Community Involvement

The teacher understands and uses a variety of instructional strategies to encourage student development of critical thinking, problem solving, and performance skills.

Closing Out the Room

Teacher Checkout Form

Teacher name _____ Room # _____

All staff members are required to complete the end-of-year tasks and duties. It is vital to a smooth opening next year that we have closure now. Below is a list of items that should be completed before you leave school. Please check with the appropriate person in your building so that you are aware of the items that should be turned in, inventoried and stored, cleaned out, and/or taken home. Thanks for your cooperation.

Item _____ Person Responsible _____ Date Due _____

Signature _____

Action	Item	Completion Date
Turned in to designated person(s)	■ Repair and summer maintenance request form	_____
	■ Grade-level supply request for startup next year	_____
	■ Summer address	_____
	■ Final retention list	_____
	■ Cumulative folders	_____
	■ Student financial obligations	_____
	■ Student information logs	_____
	■ Curriculum guides	_____
	■ Test preparation materials	_____
	■ Receipt book	_____
	■ Gradebook/lesson plan book	_____
	■ Report cards	_____
	■ Attendance cards	_____
	■ Keys	_____
	■ Staff handbook	_____
Inventoried/Stored/Secured	■ Locks	_____
	■ Textbooks	_____
	■ Teacher additions	_____
	■ Ancillary materials	_____
	■ Audiovisual equipment	_____
	■ Computers	_____
	■ Portfolios	_____
Cleaned	■ Lockers/cubbies/desks	_____
	■ Classroom	_____
	■ Teacher desk and personal materials (take home)	_____

Seminar 10 Reflections

Activity: The Year in Review

Think about the following questions.
Take time to reflect on them and the words related to
each question. Share your responses with the group.

- *What were the most memorable events of the year?*
- *What events or incidents were the most challenging?*
- *What did you do well?*

Sample words: *classroom management, conferences, lesson plans, observations,
paperwork, testing, stress, deadlines, climate, building relationships,
planning, time management*

INTASC Standard 10: School and Community Involvement
The teacher fosters relationships with school colleagues,
parents, and agencies in the larger community to
support students' learning and well-being.

Self-Assessment

"I'm Ready for Anything" Self-Assessment (Seminar 10)

How Am I Doing?	Personal Comments
What are the procedures for turning in the end-of-the-year paperwork (report cards, gradebook, attendance cards, cumulative folders, records, etc.)?	
What items must be inventoried and stored at school?	
In what condition must I leave my classroom?	
Where are textbooks and manipulatives stored?	
What types of activities are best suited for my students at the end of the year?	
How can I use my mentor and other colleagues to develop end-of-the-year activities?	
How can I best remember my students?	
What is the most difficult challenge in keeping students focused before the break?	
What type of end-of-year test or assessment is required for my content areas? How is the grade incorporated?	
How do I handle any late work or incomplete work during the last weeks?	

Seminar **11** Success and Celebrations

Contents

ONE OF MY NEW TEACHERS, IN HER FIRST
year as a middle school educator, worked with sixth-graders in a very challenging school. She began teaching with a third-grade class, but, because of licensure and certification issues, was required to move to higher grades. Her concern about "the middle grades" caused her great stress and was partly justified; changing schools, grade level, and content absolutely terrified her. We spent time discussing the characteristics of a middle school child and how different the schedule, content, and logistics of teaching would be during her first year in middle school. It is seldom that you meet someone with such total commitment to success and the desire to develop and grow, both professionally and personally.

She worked hard and took the initiative to ask questions along the way, observe and listen to others, and build strong relationships with her students. After the last seminar, she sent this note:

> *Today, I say thank you for the experience of being a part of the new teacher program! I believe that I am an effective, classroom management, cooperative learning activity, student-teacher relationship building, qualified EDUCATOR! The program made ALL the difference!"*

Introduction

Goal To reflect on the year and celebrate successes and accomplishments

Time frame Two hours

Agenda

Welcome Back and Success Stories; Concerns and Questions

Seminar 11: Success and Celebrations

Facilitator Strategies

Seminar 11 Reflections

"I'm Ready for Anything" Self-Assessment

Ready for Anything Final Evaluation

THE END OF THE FIRST YEAR OF TEACHING is a special time, and should be celebrated and recognized by all. Take time to think back and recognize the tremendous efforts made during the first year. The last seminar is a time to talk about the challenges, obstacles, successes, and professional and personal growth that each participant has experienced.

Overview

Use the assessment checklist as a last review, but make sure that this seminar is a special time for celebration, both of the success of the year and what worked with the *Ready for Anything* program. Get ready to review what you have done, even the components that you feel the most comfortable with. Take time to think about what needs revision and what the challenges have been. Make sure your teachers complete the final evaluation, so that your planning for next year's program will include their suggestions and revisions.

Preparation

Materials Chart paper, markers, tape, reproducibles (*figures 11.3–11.8*), digital photos of new teachers (framed), individual letters of commendation, refreshments

Tᴏᴅᴀʏ'ꜱ ꜱᴇᴍɪɴᴀʀ ꜰᴏᴄᴜꜱᴇꜱ on reflecting about the year and having a special time for celebration. You will need copies of the following:

- Invitation (*figure 11.1*)
- Seminar 11 Overview (*figure 11.2*)
- Reproducibles (*figures 11.3–11.5*)
- Seminar 11 Reflections (*figure 11.6*)
- "I'm Ready for Anything" Self-Assessment (*figure 11.7*)
- *Ready for Anything* Final Evaluation (*figure 11.8*)

Tip

At the end of the year, have a celebration. You deserve it!

Quote

To teach is to touch lives forever.

—Anonymous

Facilitator Strategies

Focus Reflecting on the first year of teaching.

How to Use Use the following strategies to help teachers reflect on and learn from the past year, and to celebrate their successes and accomplishments.

My Teaching Was Like A . . .

Collect a series of pictures, clip-art graphics, or objects and place them on tables for each group. Have each teacher select two graphics or objects and describe how they relate to the teacher's first year. Sample graphics include: hammer, waterfall, penny, clock, pickle, surfboard, glass, tire, doughnut, snake, apple, tin can; use others as your imagination allows. *See figure 11.3.*

"Dear First-Year Teacher" Letter of Advice

Use the letter template (*figure 11.4*) and ask your new teachers to write a letter to next year's first-year teachers. Ask them to include advice, people to talk to, helpful hints, and other ideas for success. These may be used at the first seminar of next year.

New-Teacher Award

Create an award for each of your new teachers indicating success and achievement (*see figure 11.5*). Present these at the last meeting.

Letter of Commendation

Write a letter to each new teacher commending him or her on the completion of the teacher's first year at your school. Provide a copy for the human resources employment office file.

First-Year Teacher Photo

Using photographs of your new teachers, design a collage for each teacher for the end of the year. Use a picture of the school as a background. Place the collage in a frame with the date.

Seminar 11 Reflections

Activity: A Time to Remember

Write the list of questions suggested in *figure 11.6* on chart paper and post it in the room. Ask participants to answer each question by writing a response on the chart paper. Discuss the responses with the group.

"I'm Ready for Anything" Self-Assessment (Seminar 11)

See figure 11.7.

Ready for Anything Final Evaluation

See figure 11.8.

Tip

Take time to reflect and celebrate. Challenge teachers to ask themselves, "What do I know now that I didn't know when I started?" They'll find they could each fill a book with their answers!

You Are Invited!

Seminar 11: Success and Celebrations

An understanding heart is everything in a teacher, and cannot be esteemed highly enough. One looks back with appreciation to the brilliant teacher, but with gratitude to those who touched human feeling

—Carl Jung

Date
_____

Time
_____

Location
_____

You Are Appreciated! You Made It!

- *Lots of Good Food* ▪ *Fun* ▪ *End-of-Year Surprises*
  - *Official End-of-Year Celebration*

Reflections

- Bring your best success story from the past year!

Overview

Seminar 11: Success and Celebrations

Goal

To reflect on the year and take time to celebrate successes and accomplishments.

Focus

Today's seminar focuses on reflecting about the past year and sets a special time for celebration.

Agenda

Welcome Back and Success Stories; Concerns and Questions

Seminar 11: Success and Celebrations

- Facilitator Strategies
  - My Teaching Was Like A . . .
  - "Dear First-Year Teacher" Letter of Advice
  - New-Teacher Award
  - Letter of Commendation
  - First-Year Teacher Photo

Agenda *(Continued)*

Seminar 11 Reflections

"I'm Ready for Anything" Self-Assessment

Ready for Anything Final Survey

My Teaching Was Like A...

Dear First-Year Teacher

Dear First-Year Teacher,

Here are some tips that may help you
survive your first year. Best of luck!

Sincerely, with great hope for success,

New-Teacher Award

You Made the Difference!

Way to Go!   Great Job!
CONGRATULATIONS!

First-Year Teacher Award

_____

_____

_____

Thank You!

Seminar 11 Reflections

Activity: A Time to Remember

Take time to share your answers with others
who have made it through the first year. Celebrate your
successes and get ready to look to next year.

Sample Questions:

- *What has been the most challenging part of the year?*
- *What will you do differently next year?*
- *What were the main benefits of the* Ready for Anything *seminars?*
- *What do you know now that you wish you had known when you started?*
- *What do you feel was your greatest success?*
- *What advice can you give next year's new teachers at your school?*
- *What is your favorite memory of the past year?*
- *Who provided the most support during the past year?*
- *Will you return next year?*
- *Is teaching for you?*

Self-Assessment

"I'm Ready for Anything" Self-Assessment (Seminar 11)

How Am I Doing?	Personal Comments
What are my plans for next year?	
What are my plans for the summer?	
When do I want to meet with my mentor during the summer?	
What will I do differently next year?	
What is my best memory of the past year?	
Who will I never forget, and why?	
What will I be teaching next year? *What resources do I anticipate needing?*	
How do I plan to start the year?	
What was the most important thing I learned during the past year?	
Have I checked out properly and completely, with all materials returned and stored?	
Have I made arrangements to get summer phone numbers and contacts?	
Have I indicated my desire to return?	

Ready for Anything
Final Evaluation

Program Evaluation Form

Rate the following statements using

1 = **strongly disagree**   **2** = **disagree**   **3** = **agree**   **4** = **strongly agree**

_____ The program was of high quality.

_____ The content was useful and practical.

_____ The facilitator's effectiveness was high.

_____ The facilitator possessed the necessary skills and knowledge for the seminars.

_____ The facilitator had a sense of humor.

_____ The facilitator responded to my questions and needs.

_____ The facilitator was available to help and support at other times.

_____ The facilitator provided me with additional resources, if needed.

_____ The facilitator visited my classroom on a regular basis.

_____ The facilitator was confidential and professional.

_____ The facilitator communicated my needs to the principal or designee.

_____ The seminars provided time to collaborate with other staff.

_____ The *Ready for Anything* handbook was useful and appropriate.

_____ The supplemental materials were useful.

_____ The handouts were helpful and applicable to my position.

_____ The meeting time was appropriate.

_____ The refreshments were welcomed and appreciated.

_____ I would recommend *Ready for Anything* for new teachers.

The Principal's Corner

Contents

ANY OF YOU WHO HAVE HAD THE opportunity to skydive know that it is an unforgettable experience. Whether you make the decision on your own, or are encouraged by a friend, you choose to jump out of an airplane (which is functioning perfectly well) and never think twice about it. Your enthusiasm and energy are extremely high, as are your feelings of overwhelming fear and anxiety. The instructor works with you as you attend classes, learn the logistics for survival, and undergo a period of intensive practical instruction and exercises. As the plane takes off for your first jump, you can hardly contain your excitement. Finally, the door opens and the instructor yells "Jump position!" You go out on the wing, look down from 2,800 feet, and immediately question your sanity, reasoning, and courage to go through with the jump. The culmination of all the preparation and practice occurs when you leave the plane, hoping that the static line will open the chute properly and you will land safely on the ground.

> The bottom line is this: Do you recruit or retain? Is it better to have a program in place before you actually need a program? If you don't have a program that is based on best practices, your new teachers might not make it.

A NEW TEACHER IS NO DIFFERENT FROM A first-time skydiver: both need skills and knowledge to be successful. Getting through the first day of teaching is like getting through that very first jump. Maybe first-time skydivers go back up immediately for a second jump, just to see if they were really that scared. Almost all new teachers come back the next day, just to see if they really did it the first time. The critical component for skydiving success is the effectiveness of the instructor; you, as the principal, are no different in your support of new teachers.

The bottom line is this: Do you recruit or retain? Is it better to have a program in place before you actually need a program? If you don't have a program that is based on best practices, your new teachers might not make it. If the program doesn't address the developmental needs of each individual, your new teachers might not make it. If the program doesn't have a strong, unwavering commitment from you, the principal, your new teachers might not make it.

Ready for Anything: Supporting New Teachers for Success is about people, not packaged programs. It is about a truly profound passion and development of teachers in an environment that is right for children. This program recognizes that common sense might not be so common anymore, and that out-of-the-box thinking is what will make the difference for your school. Every year, the decision to recruit or retain is yours: you alone decide whether you are willing to teach someone how to effectively manage, organize, and build relationships with students.

The Principal's Role in Teacher Retention

Now that you are a principal, if you reflect back on your first day of classroom teaching, you might discover a real compassion for new teachers. Do you remember what type of support you had? Or do you remember just being assigned a room and given a key?

Many new teachers do get the opportunity to have a supportive mentor, or to take college courses that guide and direct them along the path of educational success. Nevertheless, it is the school principal who has the knowledge, resources, and responsibility to take ownership of the role as the primary influence on the success of a new teacher. Certainly, it is often the principal who has the initial responsibility for interviewing and hiring staff. It should be clear that a corresponding, long-term investment of support and collegiality will pay off with an increase in teacher retention.

New teacher surveys identify a variety of factors that contribute to teachers leaving or becoming dissatisfied with the profession: paperwork, discipline, communication, and disillusionment. One of the most common reasons why teachers leave, though, is lack of support from the administration, specifically the principal. When the principal makes a concerted effort to create conditions that support and nurture new staff, teacher retention is more likely. Many teachers remark that although tangible items are very useful in the classroom, it is personal interaction and communication with the principal that make the ultimate difference in their decision to return to or leave a particular school.

NEW TEACHERS HAVE SPECIFIED FIVE AREAS

in which the principal can positively influence their success and desire to work toward career status:

1. Having an open-door policy and making time to share and discuss issues, concerns, and successes, without fear of intimidation or retaliation.

2. Encouraging and providing professional development in needed skills and knowledge areas, particularly classroom management and instructional strategies.

3. Establishing time for planning and collaboration with veteran teachers at the same grade level as the new teacher.

4. Creating an environment that encourages celebration, safety, and professionalism.

5. Supplying the resources and giving the support needed to integrate and align new teachers with the vision and mission of the school.

How are you doing in these areas? If you think you could use some fresh ideas and new tactics, look through the next section for some suggestions.

Many teachers remark that although tangible items are very useful in the classroom, it is personal interaction and communication with the principal that make the ultimate difference in their decision to return to or leave a particular school.

The Principal's Toolbox of Strategies

This section lists a variety of ideas and strategies to be implemented throughout the year. Here are suggestions for using them:

- **Take time to review the worksheet** on "Creating a Climate for Teamwork" (*figure P.1*) and reflect on current practices within your school. What are you doing well? Where can you make improvements in new teacher support?

- **Peruse the strategy list** and choose four or five that you are willing to implement and that are within your comfort level.

- **Create an new-teacher executive committee** (which includes the *Ready for Anything* facilitator) to implement your chosen activities, locate the resources needed for implementation, and do ongoing review and assessment of the efforts.

- **Implement your own personal plan.** Include daily visits to new teachers' classrooms, opportunities to celebrate success, and never, ever giving up on the process.

- **Review and evaluate the implementation** of the strategies on a regular basis; based on new teacher and team feedback, make changes as needed.

- **Attend all seminars.** Nothing demonstrates support for a program more than the principal's attendance and active involvement.

Seminar 1 presents several strategies for introducing your new teachers to the school and other staff. Take time to participate in these and get to know your new teachers:

Welcome to Your New Home

A Scavenger Hunt of the School

The ABCs of the District

Who, What, When, Where, and How?

Looks Are Everything!

Getting It All Together

Select several of the following activities to implement during the year. Decide, based on a budget, which of the strategies you can implement and have fun doing. Whatever you choose, remember that the key to success is consistency, so maintain your plan!

Initial Welcoming Strategies

The Infamous Bucket of Goodies

Give new staff members a "bucket" full of supplies. (A large plastic file box or crate can be reused in the classroom in many ways once the goodies are used up.) Suggested items include: a bottle of water, tissue, lip balm, overhead marker pens, candy, plastic bandage strips, a sewing kit, pencils, notebook paper, colored paper clips, a hole punch, magnets, and other classroom or personal items.

The Planning Book

Provide each new staff member with a new planning and/or grade book and a short session with suggestions on how best to use it. Ask one of your veteran teachers to share best practices.

Shopping 101

If the budget allows, provide a small amount of spending money for instructional supplies and classroom decorations. Before the shopping trip, show photos of inviting, student-centered classrooms, or have several veteran teachers share their best decorating tips.

Fitting in at Home

Provide new staff members with items displaying the school logo or mascot (e.g., shirts, mugs, lunchbags, binders, pencils, mouse pads). Give these items as door prizes throughout the year.

Getting to Know You

Do a short survey asking for a list of favorites, such as snacks, sports teams, colors, pets, hobbies, authors, and other personal (but not invasive) matters. Use this list along with the maintenance strategy called "Saw This and Thought of You" several times during the year.

A Look Back in Time

Share a history of the school and the community with your new teachers. Make a chart listing a series of significant dates, including the building of the school, its opening year, two years

> Share a history of the school and the community with your new teachers. . . . Invite veteran teachers and community leaders to share their memories of or comments on major events, tragedies, and celebrations that helped to create the school and its surroundings.

ago, and multiple years past. Add photographs for each date (as appropriate and available). Invite veteran teachers and community leaders to share their memories of or comments on major events, tragedies, and celebrations that helped to create the school and its surroundings.

Billboards

Provide a set of plaques or signs for the front focus board of the classroom (one set per teacher). Include signs such as "Today's Date," "Objective," "Warm-Up Activity," "Essential Questions" and "Homework." These plaques can be handmade or produced at a local sign shop on high-strength poster board. A suggested size is 4 inches by 28 inches, with large, black, block letters on a white background. Magnetic strips, attached to the back, allow display on most whiteboards.

Stamp of Approval

Give each new staff member an ink pad and a stamp with his or her name.

Welcome to the Business

Provide business cards for each new teacher for use at conferences, parent events, and meetings. The card should include the teacher's name, the school name and logo, the teacher's telephone number at school, and his or her e-mail address.

Provide business cards for each new teacher for use at conferences, parent events, and meetings.

Maintenance Strategies

Everyone Has a Story to Tell

Provide a time at each staff meeting for several staff members to share a story about true experiences with students and their classrooms. Preface the tale-telling with a statement that no real names will be used in the stories. For participation and order, draw names at random from a bowl.

Saw This and Thought of You

Throughout the year, have your executive team collect articles, cartoons, educational quotes, and amusing pictures related to the world of teaching. Periodically give these to your new staff members.

Down and Under

Place several stickers under chairs in the meeting room prior to a staff gathering. Award door prizes to those sitting on chairs with the stickers. A partnership with a local business may allow you to distribute nice gifts and specialty items free or for a very small charge.

Candy of the Month

Many manufacturers of commercially produced candies (and other products) relate their products to educational themes. Select a "candy of the month" and place a package of that candy in each teacher's box at the beginning of the month. Design a motivational card to attach to the candy.

My Home Cooking

Hold a "What I Ate Where I Grew Up" food celebration and have staff members bring in their favorite home or childhood foods or snacks. (Check district regulations on food brought from home before doing this activity.)

Are You Here?

One of the best opportunities to visit every classroom each day comes with collecting the attendance cards. This gives you a chance to quickly observe the classroom activities, be visible, and let your teachers know that you are interested in their work. Every so often, leave a note on the teacher's desk with a positive comment.

One of the best opportunities to visit every classroom each day comes with collecting the attendance cards. This gives you a chance to quickly observe the classroom activities, be visible, and let your teachers know that you are interested in their work.

As you hold individual conferences with your new teachers, take time to share with them why they were hired. Talk about the positive characteristics that led you to hire them and what you believe are their strengths that will support the standards and expectations of the school.

Take Time for Your Feet

Find someone in your local health organization or community who will do foot massages onsite. Allow a time during a staff meeting to relax and enjoy the pampering!

Play Time

Provide the staff with a bucket or box of toys (i.e., bubbles, games, yo-yos, Silly Putty, soft darts) and time to play and interact before a staff meeting.

Give Me a Break

Each month, identify several staff members who have gone above and beyond the normal expectations of the school day. Have a drawing for "Leave Early," "Free Conference Registration," "Free Cafeteria Cookie," or "Choice of Observation Day" passes.

Chat and Chew

Hold a "Principal's Breakfast" with your new staff every other month. At the meal, hold an open discussion around a teacher-suggested set of topics or new-teacher concerns and questions.

You Were Hired Because . . .

As you hold individual conferences with your new teachers, take time to share with them why they were hired. Talk about the positive characteristics that led you to hire them and what you believe are their strengths that will support the standards and expectations of the school. Explain what talents and abilities will be needed to effectively teach the children and work collaboratively with the school community. Don't forget to say thank you for their joining your team.

Go for the Gold

Once a quarter, do team-building activities during staff meetings. Combine these with inspirational speakers, video clips, music selections, returning-student speakers, and/or goal-setting activities.

New Teachers Have Class

Make sure that your new staff members are involved in decision making and team planning. Include them in all of the school's improvement and professional development decisions. After the year gets started, ask one of your new staff to serve on the new-teacher executive committee.

Round-Robin Professional Development

Hold a professional development day each month, rather than a staff meeting. Allow teachers to sign up for and rotate through individually designed workshops in which peers share their best methods and strategies. Make sure to include your new teachers as presenters after you have identified specific strengths and skills to be shared.

A Star Is Born

Create an achievement bulletin board for staff. Display photos and comments about their contributions and achievements during the year.

You Look Marvelous!

Use a digital camera to take photos of your new teachers. Create your own backdrops for the photo using locations around the school. Print a quote and the date and place on the photo, and frame the embellished photo for an end-of-year surprise.

This Is Entertainment

Create a video or movie presentation to share at the last staff meeting. Find someone or a student-directed group that is willing to commit to this year-long process.

Make sure that your new staff members are involved in decision making and team planning. Include them in all of the school's improvement and professional development decisions.

Just Reflecting

Mr. Poole was a wonderful principal. He would listen, make thoughtful decisions, and always take time to chat and inquire as to the status quo. I was very nervous the first time he visited my classroom and did not know how he would perceive my teaching style. He stayed about 10 minutes, then smiled and left. On the desk he left a "Happy Gram" note that said, "Thanks for being here today! The children appreciate you!" At first, I was a little insulted that he would leave a cutesy note for me, a ninth-grade teacher. As it turned out, I worked with Mr. Poole for many years, and soon began to anticipate the "Happy Gram" notes—I actually sought him out if he had not visited in a while. Recently, while I was cleaning out a large box of school mementos, I found lots of "Happy Gram"s. Mr. Poole may never understand how much that little piece of paper meant to me, but I made it through many years of challenges and struggles because of those silly little notes. Thanks, Mr. Poole, for always celebrating the small successes that teachers live for daily!

Creating a Climate for Teamwork

	Where I Am with This
I visit every new teacher's classroom at least twice a week.	
I provide positive notes and comments each time I visit a new teacher's classroom.	
I have personally checked to make sure my new teachers have the necessary materials and resources.	
I allow time at staff meetings to share exemplary teaching methods and strategies.	
I set aside informal time just to meet with my new teachers.	
I have assigned a master teacher within the same grade level or content area as a mentor for each new teacher.	
I value the strengths of each staff member and use their talents for the betterment of the school.	
I give new teachers time to network and observe my master teachers, both at my school and at others. I also give them a checklist for focused observations.	
I am always looking for additional ways to support my new staff members.	
I have tried to provide a classroom and no extra duties for my new teachers.	
I have implemented several of the strategies found in *Ready for Anything: Supporting New Teachers for Success*	

Final Thoughts

As you process and review your year
using the *Ready for Anything: Supporting New Teachers for
Success* program, take time to assess the effect you have had
on your new teachers' development. Their skills and knowledge
levels have grown tremendously over the year, and I sincerely
hope that each will return to your site next year. An effective
teacher retention process takes an investment of time and
energy and a reorganization of priorities to do *what just makes
sense*. The strategies and stories in this book are merely
starting places and suggestions; every school has its own
experiences that should also be shared with beginning staff.

There is a predictable lack of predictability in the day-to-day
world of teaching. As new teachers quickly discover, "perfect"
teaching days are rare indeed. Just when you think you've seen
it all, there's always one more student or occurrence to change
your perception of teaching, and sometimes make you think that
this job is just not humanly possible. This book cannot, of course,
address all of the challenges and issues facing educators, so
I encourage you to take the time, during each seminar, to bring
in and discuss the day-to-day things that really happen in
your school.

An effective teacher retention process takes an investment of time and energy and a reorganization of priorities to do what just makes sense.

TO GET YOU STARTED, I OFFER THE following list, which includes things and events that really take place in the world of teaching. Please feel free to incorporate any or all of them, and to add your own, as you work with your staff.

You will fall in front of your students.

Kids eat glue.

Fish die; turtles live too long.

Fires set in desks burn really big, really fast.

The number of books available never equals the number of students.

Zippers and kindergartners don't match.

Snow *is a four-letter word in the South.*

Children pull fire alarms.

Kindergarten children hold peeing contests.

Parents carry guns to school.

All teachers are wrong all *of the time.*

Kids die in bus wrecks.

Teachers get kidney infections.

The worse you are dressed on Saturday, the more parents you will see.

Snakes crawl . . . fast.

Children are abused—and teachers usually can't help.

The principal does *have a birthday.*

Boys fight. Girls claw, pull, scrape, kick, bite, yell, and rip.

Kids vomit, but never in trash cans.

Words on a board are misspelled only on the day of a formal observation.

It doesn't pay to play a video without checking it first.

Teachers cuss . . . in their heads.

Architects don't talk to teachers.

Jell-O does not stick to walls.

The paper in a teacher's mailbox reproduces on its own overnight.

Never, ever leave a cup of coffee on your desk.

Cafeteria food is, well, cafeteria food.

Condoms are found during outside-the-school scavenger hunts.

Bulletin-board border does not fold well for storage over the summer.

Computers die, normally right before you hit "Save" but just after you enter all your grades.

All programs stay the same, they just change the names.

A Word from Lynn

At the end of my second year of teaching, I asked my students to write words of advice for next year's students. I took 152 notes home and read many comments, but one has remained with me for 30 years. One student wrote, "Don't step on the little blonde, she's your teacher!" I only wish I knew who had written this note, because I accepted it for all the love and admiration I hope was intended.

You can make a difference with new teachers. It is our responsibility at the school level to provide support and constructive criticism in order to develop qualified and knowledgeable educators. Though the solutions to the teacher retention problem are not to be found in any single text, assessing your school's needs and starting a program at your site is the beginning of a successful plan. I wish you the best and hope for continued success with your new teachers.

And the Outhouse . . .

It took only a moment for me to realize how serious a situation this was: I was locked in a portable toilet, miles from help, and had only a car key with me. The options of tipping the unit over, screaming, or just waiting were not viable, so I sat on the ledge and kicked with all my energy until I broke the horribly sturdy, resistant fiberglass door. I was able to slip the car key through to raise the latch and let myself out. The price of escape was several broken toes and feet that were severely bruised for months thereafter.

> It is our responsibility at the school level to provide support and constructive criticism in order to develop qualified and knowledgeable educators.

Though the solutions to the teacher retention problem are not to be found in any single text, assessing your school's needs and starting a program at your site is the beginning of a successful plan.

Don't ever put your new teachers in the position of being locked in with no hope or way out! Provide the needed support, and don't allow them to go it alone in their search for skills and knowledge.

I probably will go traveling alone again, but I will certainly *never* use a port-a-john again!

References and Resources

References

Ainsworth, L. (2003). *"Unwrapping" the standards*. Englewood, CO: Advanced Learning Press.

Ainsworth, L. (2004). *Power standards.* Englewood, CO: Advanced Learning Press.

Anderson, L. W., & Krathwohl, D. R. (Eds.). (2001). *A taxonomy for learning, teaching, and assessing:* A revision of Bloom's Taxonomy of educational objectives (Complete ed.). New York: Longman/Allyn & Bacon.

Darling-Hammond, L. (1997). *Doing what matters most: Investing in quality teaching*. New York: National Commission of Teaching & America's Future and Teachers College Press.

Ingersoll, R. M. (2003). *Is there really a teacher shortage? A research report co-sponsored by the Consortium for Policy and Education and The Center for the Study of Teaching and Policy*. Seattle: University of Washington.

Marzano, R. J., Pickering, D. J., & Pollock, J. E. (2001). *Classroom instruction that works*. Alexandria, VA: Association for Supervision and Curriculum Development.

Marzano, R. (1998). *Dimensions of thinking: A framework for curriculum and instruction*. Alexandria, VA: Association for Supervision and Curriculum Development.

Reeves, D. B. (2004). *101 questions & answers about standards, assessment, and accountability*. Englewood, CO: Advanced Learning Press.

Reeves, D. B. (2004). *101 more questions & answers about standards, assessment, and accountability*. Englewood, CO: Advanced Learning Press.

Reeves, D. B. (2004). *Accountability in action: A blueprint for learning organizations*. 2d ed. Englewood, CO: Advanced Learning Press.

Reeves, D. B. (2001). *Holistic accountability.* Englewood, CO: Advanced Learning Press.

Additional Resources

Breaux, A. L. (2003). *101 "answers" for new teachers and their mentors*. Larchmont, NY: Eye on Education.

Canter & Associates. (1998). *First-class teacher: Success strategies for new teachers*. Santa Monica, CA: Canter & Associates.

Connors, N. A. (2000). *If you don't feed the teachers they eat the students: Guide to success for administrators and teachers*. Nashville, TN: Incentive Publications.

Harvey, S., & Goudvis, A. (2002). *Strategies that work*. Portland, OR: Stenhouse Publishers.

Jensen, E. (1998). *Super teaching*. San Diego, CA: The Brain Store, Inc.

Jones, F. (2000). *Tools for teaching*. Santa Cruz, CA: Fredric H. Jones & Associates.

Kelley, W. M. (2003). *Rookie teaching for dummies*. New York: John Wiley & Sons.

Mandel, S. (2003). *The new teacher toolbox: Proven tips and strategies for a great first year*. Chicago: Zephyr Press.

Martin-Kniep, C. O. (2000). *Becoming a better teacher*. Alexandria, VA: Association for Supervision and Curriculum Development.

Marzano, R. J. (2003). *Classroom management that works*. Alexandria, VA: Association for Supervision and Curriculum Development.

McEwan, E. K. (2002). *10 traits of highly effective teachers*. Thousand Oaks, CA: Corwin Press.

Murray, B. P. (2002). *The new teacher's complete sourcebook*. New York: Scholastic Professional Books.

Reeves, D. B. (2004). *Making standards work*. Englewood, CO: Advanced Learning Press.

Rogers, S. (1999). *Teaching tips: 105 ways to increase motivation and learning*. Evergreen, CO: Peak Learning Systems.

Rutherford, P. (2004). *Why didn't I learn this in college?* Alexandria, VA: Just ASK Publications.

Rutherford, P. (2002). *Instruction for all students*. Alexandria, VA: Just ASK Publications.

Stronge, J. H. (2002). *Qualities of effective teachers*. Alexandria, VA: Association for Supervision and Curriculum Development.

Whitaker, T. (2004). *What great teachers do differently: 14 things that matter most*. Larchmont, NY: Eye on Education.

Williamson, B. (1998). *A first-year teacher's guidebook: An educational recipe book for success*. Sacramento, CA: Dynamic Teaching Company.

Wong, H. K., & Wong, R. T. (1991). *The first days of school*. Sunnyvale, CA: Harry K. Wong Publications.

Index

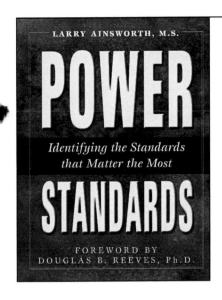

Power Standards: Identifying the Standards that Matter the Most

By Larry Ainsworth

Power Standards presents a proven process for identifying the standards that matter the most, a process that can be used successfully with every state's standards in every content area and at every grade level. The book is designed to be a step-by-step, practical manual that educators can use immediately in their own districts to replicate the process others have successfully followed.

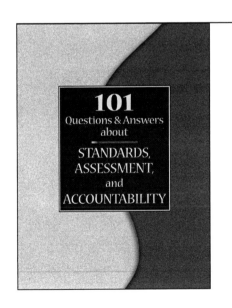

101 Questions & Answers about Standards, Assessment, and Accountability

By Douglas B. Reeves, Ph.D.

This easy-to-use reference book provides clear answers to commonly asked questions about the most pressing issues in education today. Standards and standardized tests, writing and student achievement, accountability systems, interventions for underperforming students, standards and the arts, motivation, leadership issues, plus many more topics are addressed in this handbook for educators.

These titles and more may be purchased from the Center for Performance Assessment, (800) 844-6599, or visit online at www.MakingStandardsWork.com. Also available at your local bookstore.

Do you believe all students can succeed?

Can educators make a difference and produce results?

So much to do and so little time!

Since 1992, school districts and educational organizations seeking to improve student achievement have consulted with the Center for Performance Assessment. Educational leaders on five continents have collaboratively created customized solutions based on research and results. If you would like to know more about the services of the Center for Performance Assessment, to learn about success stories in every type of educational setting, to find out about the latest research, or to arrange a presentation by a Center consultant, please visit the Web site at www.MakingStandardsWork.com or contact:

CENTER FOR
PERFORMANCE
ASSESSMENT

consulting | professional development | publishing

317 Inverness Way South, Suite 150 ▪ Englewood, CO 80112

(800) 844-6599 or (303) 504-9312 ▪ Fax (303) 504-9417